# MILITARY NECESSITY
## and CIVIL RIGHTS POLICY

Kennikat Press
**National University Publications**
Series in American Studies

MARY FRANCES BERRY

# MILITARY NECESSITY
## and
# CIVIL RIGHTS POLICY
### Black Citizenship and the Constitution, 1861–1868

National University Publications
KENNIKAT PRESS     //     1977
Port Washington, N. Y.     //     London

Manufactured in the United States of America

Published by
**Kennikat Press Corp.**
Port Washington, N. Y./London


Library of Congress Cataloging in Publication Data

Berry, Mary Frances.
  Military necessity and civil rights policy.

  (National University publications) (Series in American studies)
    Bibliography: p.
    Includes index.
  1. United States—History—Civil War, 1861–1865—Afro-Americans. 2. Slavery in the United States—Emancipation. 3. United States. Constitution—13th amendment. 4. United States. Constitution—14th amendment. 5. United States. Constitution—15th amendment. I. Title.
E453.B47     973.7'1503'96073     76-53822
ISBN 0-8046-9166-5

*TO MINERVA*

# ACKNOWLEDGMENTS

I am grateful to John W. Blassingame of Yale University, Herbert G. Gutman of the City University of New York, Francis C. Haber of the University of Maryland, College Park; James P. Shenton of Columbia University, Derrick A. Bell of Harvard Law School, Genna Rae McNeil of Howard University and William R. Leslie of the University of Michigan, all of whom read and criticized portions of this study in various forms over the years. The Civil War Round Table of Chicago awarded me essential financial support for the research. The staffs of numerous libraries, including the National Archives, the University of Michigan Law Library, and the University of Maryland, McKeldin Library, offered me invaluable assistance.

Linda B. Edwards, as in all things, made it possible for me to complete the manuscript despite encroachments on my time and energy.

Mary F. Berry

# CONTENTS

# PREFACE

The notion that one of the indicators and obligations of citizenship status was a requirement for service in the military defense of the nation influenced decisions concerning the use of blacks as soldiers throughout the antebellum period. Blacks were used reluctantly and in limited numbers in the colonial wars, the Revolutionary War, the War of 1812, and the Mexican War. The pre-Civil War experience indicated that improvement in the legal status of blacks generally, or citizenship status for black soldiers and veterans, was not a required result of the military use of blacks— at least when their efforts were not regarded as absolutely necessary for victory. But in the Civil War, the large-scale use of black soldiers was regarded by President Lincoln, the War Department, and a majority in Congress as absolutely essential to defeat the Confederacy. As a result of the enlistment of about two hundred thousand blacks in the military service, not only was it necessary for the national government to abolish slavery, but to settle the legal status of blacks generally by recognizing them as citizens. Upon achieving citizenship status, blacks could press their demands for political and civil rights, including access to public institutions and the right to vote.

Historians of the Reconstruction have elaborated a number of reasons for the adoption of the Thirteenth Amendment (which abolished slavery), including the use of black soldiers. They have also described a number of reasons for the enactment of citizenship status for blacks in the Civil Rights Act of 1866 and the Fourteenth Amendment, and the negative suffrage guarantee in the Fifteenth Amendment. John Hope Franklin, Kenneth M. Stampp, and Lawanda and John Cox have emphasized the concern of Republicans who worked for humanitarian, legal, and political equality for the freedmen. Eric L. McKitrick has suggested that the Fourteenth Amendment was a moderate civil rights measure and not radical at all. Herman Belz, William Brock, David Donald, and Charles Fairman have described the disputes over congressional Reconstruction as a compromise between groups of Republicans, and Michael Les Benedict has described the legislation as evolving from an uneasy alliance between radical and conservative Republicans, with a compromise of principle on race, which persisted until 1869. This study suggests that an additional basis for the enactment of the civil rights measures of Reconstruction originated in military enlistment policy and citizenship status definitions developed before the Civil War. Furthermore, in early 1866, when the Civil Rights Bill was enacted at a time when white soldiers were being rapidly mustered out, there were about one hundred and fifty thousand armed blacks still in the service, and millions more had been freed from bondage.

The pre-Civil War background of the relationship between eligibility for citizenship rights and military policy concerning the service of blacks is covered in this study, but the main emphasis has been placed on the Civil War experience. Throughout the entire period, however, it is clear that when military necessity compelled the widespread use of black troops, enhanced legal status for blacks resulted. When necessity became a primary factor, theories of constitutionalism and strongly held views concerning the status of persons and the limited role of government did not prevent legal improvements in the status of blacks. On the other hand, when military expediency receded, theories of the inferior legal status of blacks became again dominant.

The military case suggests that the best atmosphere in which to enact legal changes in black status is a crisis in which black reactions are perceived by whites, especially governmental officials, as having a significant bearing on the outcome. It also suggests that the attainment of blacks to the legal status of citizens was not a gift or an automatic result of principles of justice and equity in the abstract, but had to be won through sacrifice on the part of blacks and concessions on the part of whites to meet their own needs and fears. It was through military service that these adjustments in status could be negotiated.

# MILITARY NECESSITY
# and CIVIL RIGHTS POLICY

*Nothing could more strongly mark the entire repudiation of the African race. The alien is excluded, because, being born in a foreign country, he cannot be a member of the community until he is naturalized. But why are the African race, born in the State, not permitted to share in one of the highest duties of the citizen? The answer is obvious; he is not, by the institutions and laws of the State, numbered among its people. He forms no part of the sovereignty of the State, and is not, therefore, called upon to uphold and defend it.*

Justice Roger B. Taney in the *Dred Scot* case

## CHAPTER ONE

# THE COLONIAL BACKGROUND

Before a relationship between changes in the legal status of blacks and military necessity could be developed, some experience with using blacks militarily was necessary. In the American colonies in the seventeenth century, their military use appeared to be noncontroversial. The colonists, of course, placed ultimate reliance on the British fleet and soldiers to defend them from their enemies. In addition, part of the intellectual baggage that they brought to America with them included the European view that militia service was a responsibility as well as a badge of citizenship. If blacks were not citizens, they would not be permitted or expected to serve. If they were not expected or permitted to serve, that was another indication that they were not citizens. Slaves, as chattels personnel, incapable of legal marriage, property ownership, or judicial testimony, subject to the will and authority of a private or institutional owner, their labor and services totally at the disposal of others, possessed none of the attributes of citizenship status. However, unlike a machine or beast of burden, slaves were potentially capable of an infinite number and variety of services including military warfare, and it was not altogether clear at first that black person and slave would be synonymous categories. Until the end of the seventeenth century there was the possibility that blacks who were not slaves might possess the attributes of citizenship status and be expected to discharge the obligation of military service. The ambivalence and internal contradictions between racial status and slave status were reflected in the evolution of law and practice on the subject of military service.[1]

Another theme which was intertwined with the complex problem of slavery, race and military service was that of class distinctions in the character of service. In British tradition the obligation to defend one's country, or at least county, can be traced in the law in unbroken descent from the Anglo-Saxon fyrd service. The Assize of Arms in 1181, the Statute of Winchester in 1285, and their subsequent reissues, decreed the weapons which every free man must keep according to his wealth. In Elizabethan England, the worst men—poachers, thieves, and drunkards—were sent abroad in the army or navy, and more prosperous citizens stayed at home for service in the trained bands. The connection between military duty as a dignified pursuit of higher status persons who could afford to buy their own weapons and uniforms and the army abroad as fit only for undesirables persisted at the time of English colonization in America.

In England, as a result of the military role in the continuing crisis of the seventeenth century, including the Puritan Revolution and the Glorious Revolution, the distinction between categories of military service became blurred. By the eighteenth century there were just as many undesirables in the militia as in the regular army, and the upper class no longer regarded military service as its chosen profession. In the American colonies, however, consistent with their seventeenth-century origins, the distinction between home defense (the militia or National Guard) as a dignified pursuit or an obligation of the worthiest and the professional army as a place for lower classes remained.[2]

In the seventeenth century, in the American colonies as in Elizabethan England, men of the better sort were officers, and almost everyone else was in the militia. The officers were elected by their men in New England and appointed by the governor elsewhere. The militia provided their own weapons, which they kept in their homes. Indians were perceived as the real threat, and trusted blacks could generally be used to aid the settlers against them. By the end of the seventeenth century, Europeans—French and Spanish—were the new danger, but the white population had increased sufficiently to meet the new conditions. Increasingly the militia became a social organization, service in which was a hallmark of respectability or at least full citizenship in the community. However, the actual fighting in time of crisis was more often done by several classes of men who fell outside the militia structure: friendly and domesticated Indians, free blacks, white servants and apprentices, and white men on the move who were willing volunteers in search of excitement, money, and the easy discipline of army life. Respectable men were less and less willing to fight but continued to recognize a militia obligation as a badge of their freedom. A militia obligation signified citizenship status.[3]

Related to the issue of whether service was required was the issue of whether arms could be borne by certain classes of persons. Except for certain Arab states, governments have always shown extreme reluctance to allow slaves, no matter what their color, the use of arms. There was an obvious danger in permitting persons over whom one had absolute power to possess weapons. The use of arms by an organized, disciplined body of men of inferior status might create the very conditions which would promote rebellion. Such fears became even stronger when the number of slaves, as compared to the white population, increased. As the slave trade to America intensified, the distinction between bondage and freedom weakened, making *black person* synonymous with *slave*, and theories of the inferiority of blacks grew. The racial and status distinctions were made gradually and were concretized in law within the framework of the degree of military danger perceived in the unsettled conditions of the seventeenth century, including the threat of Indian attack and the competitive activities of French and Dutch settlers.[4]

The number of blacks introduced in the different colonies varied significantly and proved to be an important factor in determining the military use of blacks. There were never very many blacks in New England. In 1636 the ship *Desire* brought home the first blacks from Barbados to Salem, and thereafter in the seventeenth century blacks were brought in very rarely. But even these few were recognized as a potential threat. In Massachusetts Bay, for example, during the persistent atmosphere of crisis in the period after the successful destruction of the Pequot Indians in 1636, three statutory enactments on the subject resulted. In May 1652 the General Court provided for the enlistment of all persons in the settlement between the ages of sixteen and sixty, including blacks and even those Indians who resided with the settlers. In Connecticut at the same time blacks served in the militia. As conditions seemed less perilous some settlers expressed the view that arming Indians and blacks might be more dangerous than the uncertain advantages gained from their value in combat might justify. The Massachusetts legislature in May 1656 exempted blacks and Indians from military service. The exemption was continued through the Military Act of 1693 despite the perils in 1675 of the successful war of the New England Confederation colonists—Massachusetts Bay, Plymouth, Connecticut, and New Haven—against the Wampanoags under King Philip.[5]

With the growth and increasing visibility of the international slave trade in the last quarter of the seventeenth century, theories of black inferiority gained increasing prominence, and the process of enslavement of blacks was completed in the American colonies. By the end of the seventeenth century slavery was the presumed status of blacks throughout British America. Among New Englanders, who regarded their colonies as both commercial enterprises and little polities, slavery did not result in the mass mobilization of black workers. Blacks were objects of prejudice who could not become equal constituents of their communities but who were valuable commercial objects to be traded and sold to the Southerners and West Indians. In the South, blacks were workers who could produce wealth in a society that was not conceived as a model democracy in any case. In the middle colonies an ambivalence about motives created pockets of plantations as well as pockets where slavery was a minor feature of the landscape. But everywhere the natural condition of blacks was presumed to be slave.[6]

By 1770 in the whole New England population of ninety thousand, there were probably only a thousand blacks. However, control of these few was a matter of public concern. For example, whenever the small black population in the Massachusetts Bay colony increased by manumissions, miscegenation, and natural increase, some of the colonists expressed the view that legislation was needed to regulate their activities and to keep them from idleness and mischief. Enactments limited further manumissions unless bond of fifty pounds was given to the town treasurer, and provisions for those already manumitted had to be made by the former master. If the freedman became a public nuisance, he could be forced to labor on the public works about the town. The major emphasis of the legislation was the prevention of idleness.

There was increasing discussion of the fact that blacks were not subjected to militia duty whereas whites were. There was a recognition that requiring duty on an equal basis would contradict views concerning the inferiority of blacks and the danger of permitting them to possess arms. However, if blacks were exempted they could be argued to have the high social status of ministers, public officials, and others in the exempted classes. In 1707 the legislature found a partial solution to the problem: able-bodied free blacks were required to work on the highways and public works for as many days as the white settlers were called to give military service or to pay a fine of five shillings for each day's neglect of duty. Additionally, a statute was passed which required military service in the event of real necessity. In "case of alarm" all free blacks aged sixteen or over were ordered to report to the first commissioned officer of the town militia for whatever service might be required. Anyone who failed to report was subject to a fine of twenty shillings or eight days' labor. Throughout the period before the Revolution the legislation remained in force, and in New England blacks (whose numbers had increased to about twenty thousand, 5 percent of the total population) provided service on an individual basis in case of alarm or warfare, along with their fellow colonists. Discovered plots against whites, such as those in Hartford in 1658, in Newbury, Massachusetts, and Charleston, Massachusetts, in 1741, and a series of strange fires in Boston in 1723 served as a continual reminder of the danger of arming blacks.[7]

In the middle colonies the numbers of blacks were larger. The black population in New York increased from 2,170 out of 18,067 total population in 1698 to 19,883 out of 168,007 in 1771; in New Jersey there were 2,581 blacks out of 32,422 total population in 1726 and 4,606 out of 56,797 in 1745. In Pennsylvania there were about 2,500 blacks in 1721 and 10,274 in 1790.

In New York, where there was the largest number of blacks, there were insurrections and rumors of insurrection, such as the fully organized one in 1712 when 27 slaves armed with guns, knives, and hatchets killed 9 whites and wounded 5 or 6. There was a so-called plot in 1741 when 154 blacks and 25 whites were prosecuted for conspiring to take over the government. Belief in the plot was stimulated by the war between England and Spain and fears that blacks would aid in a Spanish takeover of New York. In the middle colonies blacks were exempted from military service in keeping with the generally expressed notion of inferiority and unreliability shared by whites, but free blacks were generally placed on "alarm lists," just as in New England. Throughout the colonial period some blacks were regularly enlisted, however, as personal servants of officers on active duty.[8]

In the South by the end of the seventeenth century blacks were generally recognized as slaves, necessary labor, and inferior objects of fear and scorn. As their numbers increased, greater restrictions and sharper control mechanisms were instituted. Blacks were generally explicitly exempted from military duty and were forbidden to bear arms for any purpose. Some Southern colonial legislatures enacted laws which permitted blacks to perform combat duty in an emergency, and in Georgia slave militiamen were subjected to support duty throughout the colonial period. In South Carolina in the Yamassee War in 1715, four hundred blacks helped six hundred whites defeat the Indians. After a 1739 slave revolt and as the numbers of blacks became larger, the slaveholders became more fearful of arming slaves. The British government organized Georgia as a white buffer and sent a regiment of regulars to South Carolina to maintain defenses after 1740. When the European wars of the eighteenth century put a continual strain on Charleston, a statute was passed in 1747 which provided for the use in warfare of any slave whose master thought he could be trusted. If the slave killed an enemy he would be rewarded with his freedom. If his service was otherwise meritorious, he would be given a livery coat, a pair of red breeches, black shoes, and a black hat to be worn once a year on the anniversary of his feat during a day of complete freedom. The South Carolina militia acts of 1778 and thereafter rescinded this proposition but provided for the use of blacks by the militia as hatchetmen or pioneers.[9]

The experience of Louisiana was distinctly different from that of any British American colony and laid the groundwork for continued race problems once Louisiana became a part of the American union. A major distinction was in the different treatment accorded slaves and free Negroes. Free Negroes were more generally recognized as possible allies of the whites, which made slightly more elevated status possible for them. Louisiana's colonial history was rooted in the social history of Spain and France. In those countries the medieval tradition that a nobleman was obliged to serve his sovereign and provide him with troops was in a state of evolution by the seventeenth century. In the French army before the French Revolution, the rich and well-born could purchase commissions and raise troops in their respective provinces in time of war. Officers who made the army a career generally enjoyed an extravagant life, with fat pensions and favors from the court. However, the French Revolution established the principle of conscript service as both a badge and moral consequence of citizenship. In Spain in the seventeenth and eighteenth centuries not only could nobles who pursued an army career gain favors, but lower-status individuals could gain status by serving meritoriously in the armed forces. In the Spanish and French colonies and in Brazil, whites were outnumbered by Indians and blacks and needed all the allies they could muster. Therefore, in law, free persons of color were clearly distinguished from whites and slaves. They generally allied themselves with whites, acquiesced or participated in the slave system, and constantly emphasized their separation from the slaves. One of their most important roles was militia duty as the police arm of the slave society and as participants in warfare against external dangers. Colored militia units were organized at first to meet specific crises and would be used as laborers and on fortifications as support troops until their loyalty was clearly demonstrated. The British, in their Caribbean colonies vastly outnumbered by slaves, followed the French and Spanish pattern. Military necessity did not permit the characterization of the small free Negro population as undesirables to be excluded from service but as allies who were expected to demonstrate their loyalty to the slave regimes. Conditions and circumstances of settlement, including population ratios and the necessity for military defense, outweighed ideological considerations.[10]

In Louisiana the French, Spanish, and British Caribbean pattern became traditional and was not easily uprooted even when circumstances changed. Blacks in large numbers were first introduced into the French colony of Louisiana in 1713; 1,000 were imported by John Law's company in 1717, and thereafter increasing numbers arrived yearly. Some died, and others were reexported, so that in 1721 only 600 remained. The white population increase also as Law attempted to abide by his contract with the French government which required him to transport some 6,000 persons to the settlement. Although in 1708 the total population did not exceed 279 persons, by 1730 the total population was 7,000.[11]

In order to formalize a system of race control, Bienville, the governor of the colony, promulgated the Black Code of 1724. Although among its provisions was a measure prohibiting the possession and use of weapons by slaves, the first military use of blacks occurred in the French period. In 1727 Perier, who succeeded Bienville as governor, armed slaves and free blacks and employed them against the Chaouacha Indians. He also used blacks to garrison the fortifications about the city and sent them on forays to aid the Illinois settlements along the Mississippi in their struggle for survival. When Bienville returned to the colony in 1785, he found 45 blacks commanded by free blacks among the 589 colonial troops from New Orleans.[12]

Thus, after the military reverses of the Seven Years' War, when France transferred her title to Louisiana to Spain, blacks were already performing military service in the colony. Color and even servitude were not automatically disabling. The first Spanish governors, Antonio de Ulloa and Don Alejandro O'Reilly, were primarily concerned with gaining the loyalty of the French inhabitants for the Spanish crown. Ulloa failed, but O'Reilly succeeded by using harsh, dictatorial methods and a strong Spanish army. During the administration of Luis de Unganza, O'Reilly's successor, greater liberality toward everyone, including blacks, was evident. Although the Black Code was retained, counsel and court trials for blacks accused of crimes, even against whites, were provided. Manumission of slaves was frequently permitted, increasing the number of free blacks in the colony.[13]

When Unganza relinquished the governorship to Don Bernardo de Galvez on January 1, 1777, the legal position of black people in Louisiana was only slightly elevated beyond what existed in the colonies to the north. The social and legal status of the small number of free Negroes and larger population of slaves was circumscribed by the provisions of the Black Code. However, blacks, slave and free, were expected to perform military service. The census of May 1, 1777, revealed only a slight population increase in the colony since the French period. There were 8,381 white persons, 273 free mulattoes, 263 free blacks, 545 mulatto slaves, and 8,474 slaves. Out of this total population, only 1,956 were legally capable of bearing arms. Manpower requirements were a principal factor in the policy of permitting the service of free people of color and even slaves when necessary.[14]

Increased necessity soon compelled changes in military policy, if not attitudes, in the British colonies. In the four American wars against the French, no humanitarian ideology was at stake, and some blacks were used by the colonists. A few slaves and free blacks served as soldiers, scouts, wagoners, laborers, and servants, but the slaves generally were compelled to return to slavery as soon as the emergency was past. But even in the humanitarian ideology of the American Revolution, only slight emphasis was placed on abolition and civil rights and privileges for blacks. Even when they insisted on their own rights to liberty and property and dubbed themselves slaves to the British, only a few colonists recognized the plight of those blacks they held in servitude or quasi-free status. The American colonists were not the first people to claim political liberty for themselves while accepting bondage for others. But the atmosphere surrounding the servitude of blacks was somewhat changed by the intense reflection on human rights in the Western world in the mid-eighteenth century. Montesquieu had included a critique of slavery in the eleventh book of his *Spirit of Laws*, and several Scottish moral philosophers, including Francis Hutcheson, had been bluntly critical of slavery. Their works were widely distributed in the colonies by Quakers. A few lonely Quakers in America also initiated pleas against slavery in the 1750's. Benjamin Franklin, addressing Philadelphia leaders in *Observations Concening the Increase of Mankind* (1751), produced figures to show that slavery was uneconomical. In 1764, James Otis published his famous and widely disseminated pamphlet, "The Rights of the British Colonies Asserted and Proved," in which black slavery was explicitly arraigned before the bar of Natural Rights. Otis asked, "Does it follow that 'tis right to enslave a man because he is black?" and asserted "that the colonists black and white born here are free born British subjects and entitled to all the essential civil rights as such...."[15]

As the 1760's proceeded an antislavery movement was nascent. Such colonists as Anthony Benezet, the Philadelphia Huguenot, and John Woolman, the New Jersey Quaker, increasingly denounced English oppression, slavery, and the slave trade. The role of a black man, Crispus Attucks, in the Boston Massacre, served in part to point up the inconsistency. But protests against slavery and the slave trade were mere sideshows during the Revolutionary War. Of the thirteen colonies, the only legislature even to consider an act of emancipation between 1765 and 1780 was that of Pennsylvania. Even there the persistent efforts of Quakers and others to achieve an act of gradual abolition did not bear fruit until 1780.

In the organization of the national government during the war under the Articles of Confederation, the issue of slavery and military policy was discussed when the basis for representation and the basis for taxation and troop requisitions were before the Continental Congress. Representation, it was decided, would be based on one vote for each state on all questions. A proposal for proportional representation based on population, which would have necessitated categorizing slaves as included or excluded, was voted down. Taxation was a more difficult issue, since slaveholders would not have minded having slaves excluded from a count of taxable persons.

This problem was resolved by apportioning taxes based on land values within each state.[16]

After the Articles were submitted to the states in November 1777, several delegates questioned the racial implications of certain clauses. On the section which provided that troops for the Continental Army would be requisitioned from states in accordance with the total white population, Southerners objected that their laws required patrols of white men to prevent fugitive slaves from escaping and to protect themselves against slave insurrections. Northerners in Massachusetts, Pennsylvania, and New Jersey retorted that requisitions should be based on total population and that it was a concession to permit Southern states to draw only on the white population. The delegates in these states asserted that the Declaration of Independence meant that all persons should contribute equally to defense. They apparently had no intention of continuing automatically to exclude blacks from the service although "necessity and experience" might justify some states in refusing to arm some inhabitants. These three states were the only ones to vote in favor of removing the word *white* from the clause. Such a change in racial attitudes as well as attitudes toward the military use of undesirables was too far advanced for the Southern states. South Carolina apparently feared that some states would abolish slavery as part of revolutionary objectives because their delegates, with the support of one other state, Georgia, suggested that the privileges and immunities clause be amended to include only white inhabitants as the beneficiaries of of privileges and immunities in the several states. Eight states voted against this change in the interest of not having to submit the Articles to the states again. Additionally, Article 2 of the Articles of Confederation, as adopted, recognized the retention of state control over domestic institutions including the institution of slavery.[17]

As the struggle between Parliament and the Americans resulted in actual warfare, what to do with the blacks became a great concern. The population of the thirteen colonies was 2.5 million people, and one-fifth were blacks—90 percent of whom lived in the Southern colonies and 90 percent of whom were slaves. In Virginia blacks were 40 percent of the population, in South Carolina blacks were one-half of the population; but along the coast, in areas more vulnerable to attack, they outnumbered whites by as much as ten or twelve to one. In any extended warfare and in any ensuing peace, the disposition of the blacks would have to be taken into account. Before waiting for the issues to be debated, blacks joined the fighting from the beginning. On April 18, 1775, when the expedition sent by General Horatio Gates to Lexington and Concord returned to Boston, militiamen fired upon the Redcoats all along the route. There were black volunteers long used to service "in case of alarm" among the militiamen who hurried to join the fray.[18]

During the next month the Continental Congress passed a considerable body of legislation to support the war. In the crisis atmosphere no effort to exclude blacks or any other class of persons from military service was recorded. To prosecute the war effectively, Congress considered means of acquiring gunpowder and stores and resolved to form companies of expert riflemen to join the undisciplined militia forces encamped around Boston.[19]

Congress also had to consider the matter of choosing a commander in chief. It seemed that New England might have first claim, since their region was under fire and had provided most of the militiamen. However, it was decided that because John Hancock had been elected president of the Congress as a concession to New England, it was time for the South to receive some consideration. George Washington of Virginia was appointed and directed to proceed to Cambridge and organize the forces there into the Continental Army under his command.[20]

On June 24, 1775, Congress received word of the Battle of Bunker Hill. In that battle, black militiamen, some of whom had been at Lexington and Concord, again fought with the volunteer forces. There was a sprinkling of black soldiers in almost every New England company in the early months of the war. Some were slaves who enlisted with the consent of their masters; others were free blacks who simply volunteered in the first rush of local enthusiasm for the war.[21]

In response to the news concerning the war in New England, Congress began to prepare legislation for the organization of the Continental Army. On June 30 the delegates approved sixty-nine articles of war for the governance of the American Army and prepared a pay scale for officers and men. In order to provide funds for the payment of the army and prosecution of the war, the Congress began to issue paper money, and a resolution was passed calling upon each colony to provide ways and means of supporting its proportion of the paper currency that was issued. Quotas or proportions for each colony would be determined according to the number of inhabitants of all ages, including blacks. Before adjourning, Congress recommended the formation into militia companies of all able-bodied males between the ages of sixteen and fifty years. The legislation made no mention of race or color.[22]

Black volunteers fought at Lexington and Concord, and at Bunker Hill, but the door was soon shut to their general enlistment. After the immediate crisis had passed, the issue of the obligation of military service of blacks came to the forefront, since they were regarded as property, a possibly disruptive force and incapable of citizenship. The army's own authority decided to exclude them. On July 10, 1775, General Horatio

Gates, the army adjutant, issued an order to recruiting officers forbidding the enlistment of blacks, among other undesirables.[23]

The tendency throughout the wars of the seventeenth and eighteenth centuries had been to collect volunteers, including friendly Indians, a few Christians, and large numbers of idle, dissolute people to fight the colonial wars. The better people had been less and less willing to fight. But the Revolutionary War was seen, at first, by the patriots as the occasion for the revival of the reliable militia and not an occasion for the use of the undesirable volunteers with no real stake in the community. Blacks, were, of course, considered among the undesirables. By the time Congress reconvened on September 26, the crisis had intensified; but Edward Rutledge, who was described by a fellow delegate as speaking "through his nose like the Yankees sing, with-out much force or effort," proposed the discharge of all blacks from the service. This was in keeping with the generally accepted notions of black inferiority and the inordinate fear of blacks in South Carolina, which was reflected in the slave code prohibition of the use of arms by blacks. But some blacks were already fighting among the patriot troops, and the crisis was real. Rutledge's motion was lost.[24]

On September 29 the Congress appointed a committee to go to Cambridge for conferences with Washington and the local representatives of the committees of safety in New England. The conference was to consider means of supporting and regulating the Continental Army. The patriarch of the Congress, Benjamin Franklin, Thomas Lynch, a delegate from South Carolina, and Benjamin Harrison of Virginia were appointed to the committee. They went to Cambridge, where they stayed for ten days, discussing, among other matters, whether the crisis warranted continued black enlistments. The conference adopted a policy of exclusion of free blacks as well as slaves. They did not believe conditions necessitated a change in long-standing policy or that blacks would be disciplined, reliable troops. The army headquarters at Cambridge issued orders to this effect at least twice in October and posted an order to confine any blacks found "straggling" near the army encampments between sunrise and sunset.[25]

Blacks who were already in the service and who understood the opportunity for improved legal status that might result were firmly opposed to the policy of exclusion, and they took their complaints to Washington's headquarters. Washington wrote to Congress on December 31, 1775, seeking advice on the problem. The situation was grave, because Washington's small army was threatened with extinction by the approaching expiration of the terms of service of many militiamen. Furthermore, the British offer, through Lord Dunmore's proclamation of November 1775 to give slaves of rebels their freedom in exchange for military service and to accept any free black or slave who volunteered left the way open for blacks to join the British forces. Any slave who heard of the proclamation and wanted to take his chances on the ultimate outcome of the war and the earnest intentions of the British could run away and join their forces. The proclamation was not as threatening as it seemed at first glance, because the British did not embark on a policy of general emancipation and seemed reluctant to recruit large numbers of blacks out of racial prejudice and an intention to reestablish the status quo instead of precipitating an internal social revolution. Furthermore, the British army had enough trouble training and disciplining loyalist recruits and would have found it extremely difficult to induct and train large numbers of black soldiers in order to use them efficiently. Additionally, the British knew that many at home would regard with disfavor a rebellion of whites suppressed by armed blacks. British reluctance allied with hesitation on the part of Northern whites served to neutralize the issue. The Continental Congress considered the manpower problem but on January 16, 1776, decided to permit the retention of those free blacks who had already served faithfully. No other black volunteers would be accepted.[26]

The provincial legislatures agreed with the policy of Congress. The Massachusetts General Court passed an act on January 22 excluding blacks, Indians, and mulattoes from ordinary service. Further legislation exempted such persons from even the alarm lists, thus repealing the statute of 1707. Statutes resembling the Massachusetts law were passed in the other provincial legislatures. At the time of the signing of the Declaration of Independence, blacks were statutorily exempt from combat duty in all the former colonies. Some Southern provinces, such as Virginia and South Carolina, had limited provisions for the service of blacks as musicians, pioneers, and hatchetmen. Some Northern provinces continued to enlist blacks surreptitiously in spite of prohibiting statutes.[27]

In the summer of 1776 the American military future seemed bright. The Canadian campaign had been the only real setback, and the news of the British repulse at Charleston on July 4 merely enhanced the jubilation. However, during the next few weeks the British arrived with a startling array of warships and an expeditionary force of some 34,000 men, including Hessian mercenaries. The American army appeared, wrote Lord Howe's secretary, Ambrose Serle, to be a motley collection of ragged old men, boys, "and blacks of all ages."[28]

In the autumn of 1776 the British simply ran the militiamen out of New York. It was immediately obvious that more stringent military measures were required. In order to encourage long-term enlistments, Congress unsuccessfully offered bounties and land to recruits. During the fall and winter military matters worsened. Congress passed numerous resolutions calling upon the states for greater efforts in providing manpower, arms, and equipment for prosecuting the war. The military reverses continued throughout 1777, until Washington's defeat at Brandywine on September 11 forced Congress to flee to York. As the Congress made more pressing demands on the states, blacks were at first covertly and then overtly taken into the service. In January 1778, the Massachusetts legislature responded to a call for fifteen regiments for the Continental Army by passing a resolution subjecting everyone except Quakers to military service. Another resolution, passed in April, legally sanctioned the enlistment of blacks.[29]

Increasingly, the lack of available manpower plagued the American effort. During the winter at Valley Forge, diseased, unpaid, underclothed, undernourished, and racked by desertions, Washington's army seemed on the point of dissolution. General James Varnum of Rhode Island suggested that a black battalion be recruited in his state, then two-thirds occupied by the British. Washington sent Varnum's memo to the governor of Rhode Island, urging that his state do everything to meet its quota of troops set by Congress. An act was passed in Rhode Island in February 1778 providing that slaves who enlisted would be freed and their masters paid up to one hundred twenty-five pounds. The black battalion recruited on this basis fought for five years in the battle for independence. The act was passed because "for the preservation of the rights and liberties of the United States it is necessary that the whole power of government should be exerted in recruiting the continental battalions." They would be paid wages equal to those received by white soldiers and given a certificate of freedom at the end of the war.[30]

By the end of 1778, Congress and the army were even more prepared to take any men they could get. The distinction between desirables and undesirables for military service was becoming increasingly blurred. When the British marched into Georgia and captured Savannah in March 1779, the South Carolina legislature, fearing that an invasion was imminent, besought the Congress for increased military aid. A Continental Congress committee report on defense in the Southern states concluded that few effective efforts could be made "by reason of the great proportion of citizens necessary to remain at home to prevent insurrections among the negroes, and to prevent the desertion of them to the enemy." In this atmosphere of crisis, John Laurens, a former aide-de-camp to Washington and now a lieutenant colonel, pressed his plan for the enlistment of slaves. Laurens was the son of Henry Laurens, a wealthy South Carolina merchant and president of Congress from November 1777 to December 1778. Young Laurens believed that black slaves could be bought from their masters and enrolled in the Continental Army. They could be put under army discipline both for defense and to lessen the possibility of revolt. After the war the slaves would be freed and given a bounty of fifty dollars. In the emergency, William Drayton, the other representative from South Carolina, supported the elder Laurens in trying to convince Congress of the efficacy of the plan. Henry Laurens felt that Washington's support might influence a Congressional decision, so he wrote to the general asking for a favorable opinion. Washington replied that he had not given the matter much thought, but he thought that the emancipation and arming of slaves would create discontent among those left in bondage. On March 14, 1779, in a letter to John Jay, president of the Congress, Alexander Hamilton, then a young colonel in the Continental Army, offered his support of the plan. The Southerners were faced with fear of the British, fear of insurrection, the need for blacks to continue as slaves to maintain the plantation system, and fear of improving the possibility of general abolition or emancipation through training an additional coterie of blacks in warfare. They decided that the best course of action was to insist upon more support from the Continental Army in the North and to oppose projects to arm blacks. Even if the British won, the system of slavery would continue.[31]

On March 29 Congress, noting the approval of the South Carolina delegation, recommended that Georgia and South Carolina enlist three thousand able-bodied slaves into battalions staffed by white officers. The slaves would be purchased from their masters for one thousand dollars each, and would be given their freedom and a bounty of fifty dollars at the end of the war. John Laurens was sent by the Congress to South Carolina to present the plan to the Assembly there. The South Carolina Assembly firmly rejected the plan, and, although Laurens tried again three years later, general slave enlistment for armed military duty was never accepted by the South.[32]

General Nathaniel Greene of Rhode Island, who was sent in 1780 to reorganize the forces there, continued efforts to convince the lower South of the efficacy of raising black troops. He complained constantly about the inadequate manpower and equipment available for the army. Even after Yorktown, Greene continued his efforts. In January 1782 he wrote to Washington describing the abject condition of his men who "were almost naked for want of overalls and shirts," and expressing his disgust at the behavior of states that did not accede to the requisitions of Congress. Greene thought that the difficulties of the Continental Army would increase until "the powers of Congress are more extensive, and the subordination of the States is better acknowledged." He thought that Congress could make requisitions "until they were blind and the local policy of the States in perfect security will counteract our wishes." He suggested a stoppage of trade in "disagreeable" states. Greene informed Washington of his continuing efforts to convince the South to raise black regiments. They could not enlist sufficient numbers of white men locally, and because of "prejudices" respecting the climate, it was difficult to obtain reinforcements from the North.[33]

Generally, until the end of the war, the lower South refused to arm blacks, slave or free. Virginia and South Carolina, however, retained a provision for the service of some blacks as laborers or pioneers. Hard-pressed Maryland in 1780 authorized the enlistment of slaves and free blacks. Above the Potomac, however, after 1778, blacks were enlisted increasingly everywhere as substitutes and as volunteers in the army. Blacks, who had few options in civilian life, were more willing to serve for longer periods than whites and rarely deserted. Furthermore, in keeping with long-standing attitudes toward status differentiation in the military, when blacks served in the Continental Army whites could be given shorter enlistments and remain at home for home defense. An official return of the Continental Army for August 1778 listed 755 known blacks in the service even at that time. The pension rolls and war records of the various states contained evidence of black enlistment throughout the remaining years of the war.[34]

During the Revolutionary War, important aid to the American cause, including the use of black troops, came from an unexpected source. Don Bernardo de Galvez and the Spanish colony of Louisiana strongly supported the rebel effort in the South with military aid performed, in the main, by militia companies which included blacks, although initial assistance given by the Spanish consisted largely of supplying gunpowder and stores. Upon the advent of his term of office as governor, on January 1, 1777, Galvez continued to supply the Americans with small quantities of these valuable supplies. He also lent a sympathetic ear to the plans of American revolutionaries in New Orleans for expeditions against British-held Pensacola. The English were not unaware of Galvez's association with the Americans. As early as March 1777 the British governor of West Florida protested to the Spanish government. Although Spain was still neutral, Galvez continued to aid the Americans by sending supplies to George Rogers Clark and his western army and by expediting American shipping along the Gulf and up the Mississippi. This aid was an integral part of the Spanish policy of opposing the English all along the Mississippi River.[35]

Galvez gave direct assistance to James Willing's expedition in 1778. Willing, a Natchez merchant with close family connections in Philadelphia, was a self-styled revolutionary agitator. Willing went to Philadelphia in the fall of 1777, where he presented a plan to proceed by boat down the Ohio and the Mississippi, obtain aid and supplies from the Spanish at New Orleans, and march to West Florida. There, with the aid of a simultaneous sea bombardment, he would force the English to withdraw. Henry Laurens of

South Carolina regarded the plan as ridiculous in the face of impending danger to Philadelphia, which required all the military effort which could be mustered; but he reported that the idea was adopted by a "few within [the Congress] and apparently acquiesced in by a great majority."[36]

The Willing expedition set out on a series of raids along the Mississippi frontier, driving British refugees into Spanish Louisiana in front of them. Galvez officially adopted a policy of neutrality both toward the refugees and Willing's party, which came in afterward. In fact, however, he protected the Americans and their prizes, which were taken from the British and brought into port at New Orleans. The Continental Congress was greatly pleased with Galvez's attitude and expressed their warm appreciation for his disregard of British protests against his action.[37]

Since he was courting attack from the British by helping the Americans, and the colony was in poor shape militarily with a small population at the beginning of his administration, Galvez found it necessary to strengthen the defenses of New Orleans. He succeeded in improving the naval fortifications and doubling the size of the militia. In June of 1779, after Spain had declared war against England, Galvez was expected to use military force, over and above the aid and secret diplomacy exercised during the period of neutrality. In preparation for war Galvez held a council of his principal advisors to whom he described the critical situation of Louisiana. There were only 650 Spanish regular troops in the colony, so that greater reliance had to be placed on the militia. Instead of waiting for a British attack, Galvez decided to act aggressively. After providing as well as possible for the defense of New Orleans, he set out on August 27 on an expedition against Pensacola. His army consisted of 170 Spanish regulars, 330 recruits from Mexico and the Canary Islands, 20 carabineros, 60 militiamen and habitants, 8 free blacks and mulattoes, and 7 American volunteers. He recruited some 760 more men, whites, blacks, mulattoes, and Indians along the way, making a total of 1,427 men.[38]

Although this force was nearly decimated by illness, he successfully laid siege at Baton Rouge against 650 English troops, including some blacks. On September 21, 1779, the English surrendered their forts at Baton Rouge and Natchez. Galvez then returned to New Orleans to prepare for a larger expedition against Mobile, which had to be taken before Pensacola could be captured. On January 2, 1780, he was finally able to set out for Mobile. His force consisted of 234 regulars, 14 artillerymen, 36 carabiniers, 323 white militiamen, 107 free black and mulatto militiamen, 24 slaves, and 26 Americans, strongly supported by a number of ships. On May 14, 1780, he captured the fortress at Pensacola, whereupon the British surrendered the entire province of West Florida. The conquests of Galvez were important, not only for West Florida, but for the entire Mississippi Valley, because they influenced the English decision from St. Louis in May 1780. The British plan had called for an expedition from Canada, down the Mississippi, coordinated with an attack from the South, which Galvez's success prevented. The Spanish were interested in inhibiting the British, and the utilization of black manpower was one necessary aspect of a successful Spanish policy that gave valuable aid to the American Revolution.[39]

The Revolutionary War required the use of black soldiers by Louisiana and the Northern provinces in the struggle for independence. Some slaves were manumitted either upon enlistment or at the end of their service for service in the patriot army. The fact that as soon as Cornwallis surrendered at Yorktown Washington ordered sentinels posted along the beach to prevent blacks from stowing away aboard British vessels gives some indication that the end of slavery generally was not in view with the successful conclusion of the war. Article VII of the Treaty of Peace, which guaranteed that the British army woud leave in the United States slaves or other property belonging to the Americans, formalized the intentions that a large-scale exodus of black people in search of freedom would not be permitted. There had been some delegates to the Continental Congress who regarded the Revolution as a blow for slaves' freedom as well as their own; military officers like Laurens and Hamilton had been willing to strike for emancipation when it was combined with local military necessity. Blacks themselves had petitioned unsuccessfully to state legislatures for their freedom in the name of natural rights and military service. However, the presence of a few blacks in the army and their emancipation could not provide a basis for improving the legal condition of blacks in all areas of the country. The inconsistency in principle had been highlighted, but the value and importance of slave property as well as racial attitudes and the necessity for race control were countervailing factors.

The Revolutionary War taught blacks that when a war could be, and was, won without the necessity for large-scale use of black troops, only limited improvements in the status of blacks would be made. In New England, where blacks were few, where black petitioners articulated their concerns, where blacks provided the greatest assistance to the war effort, and where the comparative disadvantages of abolition were smallest, within a year of the Revolution some provision for the abolition of slavery had been made. The natural rights philosophy of the Revolution bore abolitionist fruit more easily under such conditions. In Massachusetts, in the ambiguous Quok Walker and Nathaniel Jennison cases and their progeny before the Supreme Court of Judicature, in New Hampshire and Vermont in the state constitutions, and in Rhode Island and Connecticut by statute, slavery was put on the way to gradual extinction. As a result, the 1790 census reported only 3,763 slaves among the 16,882 blacks in New England; by 1810 there were only 418—108 in Rhode Island and 310 in Connecticut. Pennsylvania's gradual abolition act was passed in 1780. Revolutionary ideology and prerevolutionary antislavery activity, unfettered by the presence of large numbers of blacks, made limited abolition possible. But there were still 11,000 slaves in New Jersey and 21,000 in New York as the Revolutionary period moved to a close, and slavery was still deeply entrenched where the majority of slaves were, in the South. The ideology of the Revolution was an insufficient basis for supporting widespread abolition, and military necessity was not great enough to tip the balance toward large-scale freedom. The few scattered black troops set free and given training in the North were not a threat to the maintenance of the institution in the South.[40] Since no pressing military necessity was demonstrated, the Revolutionary War experience left open the question of whether military expediency could tip the balance toward general abolition and improvement in the legal status of blacks.

## CHAPTER TWO

# MILITARY SERVICE FOR

# WHITE MALES ONLY

On the subject of the liability of certain categories of males for military service, white American attitudes did not change significantly as a result of the War for Independence. In the South, more than ever, the notions that militia service was a privilege and obligation of citizenship for white males, and that service in the officer corps was a dignified occupation for gentlemen, persisted. The notion of service itself would be degraded by utilizing such inferior creatures as blacks. Furthermore, arming blacks was still an obvious danger to the institution of slavery. The greater the number of blacks the more likely was insurrection regarded as a possibility. Outside the South, the eighteenth-century English recognition that militia service, even for officers, had declined in status was more obvious; but there was still lingering sentiment that compulsory long-time service was for the off-scourings of humanity and that the good people, sturdy workmen and worthy burghers, could be called upon for home defense. Blacks, even when freed in the Revolutionary War, were still treated as political and social unequals, even as compared to poor whites. The long-held conviction that the African race was inferior and the white superior was not erased from the public mind. The United States was a white man's country, and the laws on military service reflected that view. Everywhere the position that during times of crisis the extent of the crisis itself would determine the acceptance or nonacceptance of volunteers, and that even blacks might be accepted if the necessity was pressing, was generally acknowledged.

When the exigencies of union made it necessary to draft a new constitution for the United States, military provisions which reflected decisions about the status of blacks were made. The chief issues to be resolved in forging a constitution for a nation instead of a conglomeration of states were the same ones that had been unsuccessfully resolved in the Articles of Confederation—representation, taxation, and regulation of trade and commerce. According to James Madison, on the issue of representation there was a significant division among the states resulting from a difference of circumstances. "The most material of which resulted partly from climate, but principally from the effects of their having or not having slaves. These two causes concurred in forming the great division of interests in the United States. It did not lie between the large and small states; it lay between Northern and Southern." Having or not having slaves was a major factor in determining state interest in the outcome of the Constitutional Convention.[1]

By the time the convention met, there was a consensus among politicians that the slaveholders would insist that whatever formula of representation was devised, it must provide some representation for slaves. When the Articles of Confederation provision that taxation would be based on land values in each state was found unworkable because there was no valuation on which everyone could agree, an unsuccessful attempt was made to amend the Articles to base taxation on population rather than land values. In 1777 Benjamin Harrison of Virginia suggested that slaves be calculated at half the value of free men, but New Englanders refused to concur, insisting that slaves should be counted at full value. The New England position was based on opposition to decreasing the South's tax burden and not on recognition of the dignity and worth of slaves as individuals. In 1783 a congressional committee on public credit presented a proposal again to base taxation on population. This time a compromise proposal that three slaves be counted as five freemen was rejected by the states when submitted for ratification along with a number of other reforms designed to amend Article 8. The unanimous vote required to amend the Articles of Confederation could not be garnered. However, the three-fifths ratio was an idea that had gained general acceptance by the time the Constitutional Convention met. The inclusion of the three-fifths compromise in the Constitution for both purposes of representation and taxation gave sanction to the notion that the United States was composed of free and unfree persons and was a clear acknowledgment of the legality of slavery and racial inequality and the power of slavery's defenders.[2]

The adoption of the Fugitive Slave Clause and the military clauses of the Constitution gave further evidence of the legality and acceptance of slavery and racial inequality. There was little debate on the Fugitive Slave Clause, which in itself indicated the general agreement on the issue. On the military clauses it was clear that instead of regarding blacks as part of any military forces, in fact militias and the national forces could ultimately be expected to suppress slave insurrection. The Three-Fifths Clause, the Fugitive Slave Clause, and the military clauses were used as definite selling points by supporters of the Constitution in Southern ratifying conventions. George Nicholas in the Virginia convention emphasized the additional security provided for slavery. Along with the power of the state to use its military to control the slaves, "it will be the duty of the general government to aid when the strength of the union is called for." James Madison particularly emphasized the usefulness of the Fugitive Slave Clause in Virginia as did some of the Federalists in the North Carolina convention. Furthermore, even on the question of why the Constitution contained no Bill of Rights, the slavery issue was utilized by supporters of ratification. Charles Cotesworth Pinckney explained to the South Carolina convention that "such bills generally began with declaring that all men are by nature born free. Now, we should make that declaration with a very bad grace, when a huge part of our property consists of men who are actually born slaves." It was entirely proper to make such an assertion in a general declaration such as the Declaration of Independence but not in a constitution embodying enforceable, fundamental law. The antislavery forces in the Constitutional Convention focused all of their fire on obtaining a clause for prohibiting the slave trade and gained an agreement that Congress could not prohibit the trade until 1808. Slavery forces obtained the commitment of the national government to protect slavery, but not interfere with it, as an indispensable part of the Constitution.[3]

Early congressional legislation implementing the provisions of the Constitution in order to establish the new government reflected the popular conception of the racial inequality of blacks enshrined in the Constitution. In 1790 Congress passed the Naturalization Act, which extended the privileges of citizenship to all free white persons. In 1794 and early 1795, during consideration of amendments to the act, Federalist Samuel Dexter of Massachusetts suggested that aliens be required to renounce possession of slaves forever before being naturalized. His suggestion was a reaction, in part, to the proposal of William Giles of Virginia to include a clause requiring aliens to renounce all claims to titles of nobility, an issue that was of interest primarily to Federalists with aristocratic pretensions. In the debate, James Madison and Giles indicated that Virginians were in favor of getting rid of slavery as soon as possible but did not feel that the subject should be discussed prematurely in public. Madison said that "the mention of such a thing [the possibility of ending slavery] in the House had in the meantime a very bad effect on that species of property [slaves]. It has a dangerous tendency on the minds of these unfortunate people." Otherwise, he would have voted for Dexter's amendment. The result was that twenty-eight congressmen, all Northerners except William Vans Murray of

Maryland, Giles's old foe, voted in favor of Dexter's motion, which was defeated sixty-three to twenty-eight. Giles's motion as approved meant a refusal to limit the legitimacy of slavery.

In organizing the militia in 1792, Congress restricted enrollment to white male citizens between the ages of eighteen and forty-five, each of whom would provide his own musket, freelock, bayonet, or other arms, and equipment. The Constitution gave Congress the power to make rules and regulations for the militia, leaving to the states only the power to appoint the officers and train the militia. States could legislate on the subject but only under the paramount authority of Congress. When Congress restricted service to white male citizens as part of its organizing authority, this precluded the states from including blacks in official militia organizations. The act to organize the army, navy and marines passed on April 30, 1790 did not have a racial clause, but in 1798 the secretaries of War and Navy issued separate directives forbidding black enlistments in the Marine Corps and on naval warships. However, black sailors continued to be used on naval vessels when commanders thought it necessary. Some served prominently and often courageously during the Naval War with France (1798-1800) and the War of 1812.

Although the failure to legislate blacks out of the regular forces might, at first glance, seem inconsistent or an indication of enlightened racial views, there were two reasons for this exception. The distinction between militia duty as the first line of defense and the standing, or permanent, army and navy, whose forces could be augmented in time of crisis, was still clearly accepted during the late eighteenth and early nineteenth centuries. The regular army or navy was a place for undesirables, and during a war manpower would be drawn for it from any readily available source under the Constitutional power to raise and support armies. The militia was both a social and military organization during peace time and the first line of home defense as well as a mechanism for slave control. Furthermore, not every able-bodied citizen was required to serve in the regular forces, and such service was not a badge of citizenship. The concept of militia duty would have been distorted by including blacks; but the concept of regular service was not distorted by including no race or class restrictions whatsoever.[4]

Some members of Congress during the period before the War of 1812 occasionally made clear their understanding of these distinctions. In January 1793 the issue was raised in a discussion of defense of the Northwest frontier—the ambush of General Josiah Harmer and fifteen hundred militiamen in 1790 and the 1791 expedition of Governor Arthur St. Clair of the Northwest Territory and his two thousand ill-equipped and untrained men, who either deserted or were trapped and forced to flee for their lives.

When the Congress determined to arm and equip a militia force for a successful 1795 campaign, in the debate traditional views were expressed concerning the reliability of militia as opposed to regular forces. Josiah Parker explained that the regular army was "collected from the stews and brothels of the cities, and had none of the spirit or principles of the honest yeomanry who comprised the militia in former wars." John Steele of North Carolina agreed with him, saying "it would give me pain to describe the trash which comprises all regular armies. They enlist for three dollars a month, which in a country like the United States, is a sufficient description of their bodies as well as their minds." The vote was very close, thirty-six to twenty, but most members were persuaded that there were not enough honest militiamen on the frontier to defeat the Indians, and they must continue to support the regular army.

In 1795, when considering amendments to the Militia Act, an unidentified member moved to strike out the white-only clause. Aaron Kitchell of New Jersey said he hoped that if the word *white* was struck out, *black* would be inserted, as "it was necessary that the militia should all be of one color. White men would not stand in the same rank with a Negro." Another member said that "he was not for a speckled militia." A member from a Southern state, apparently Madison, said that "the subject was obviously and extremely improper for public discussion," and reminded the House that he had warned them against discussion of slavery and the status of blacks when they were considering Dexter's motion on the Naturalization Act. The amendment was voted down.[5]

After state legislatures passed militia laws which expressed the racial exclusion principle of the federal statute in the period after the Revolution, only in Louisiana were blacks permitted to serve in the legally constituted militia. Louisiana free people of color held fast to their tradition of service, firmly established by men who had fought in the army of Galvez. When the United States purchased Louisiana from France in 1803, there were some 1,768 slaves and 22,444 white persons. There were three companies of free people of color, comprising 300 men. The free people of color enjoyed by law some of the advantages enjoyed by whites, and the Treaty of Purchase assured the continued existence of these rights.

William C. Claiborne, the young, successful former congressman from Tennessee and governor of the Mississippi Territory, who was appointed as the first governor of the Louisiana Territory, found Louisiana to be in a potentially explosive situation. There was a major problem of consolidating the loyalty and support of a heterogeneous population: some had ties to the French, others to the Spanish, and all were noticeably annoyed by the transfer of the territory to the United States. In the area around New Orleans, it was feared that a highly incendiary situation might develop because the large-scale immigration of blacks from Cuba and Santo Domingo had rapidly increased the number of free blacks. The governor expected the free colored population to show its enmity toward the United States on the occasion of the public transfer ceremonies, and he requested extra arms and ammunition from President Jefferson. There was no demonstration. The militia corps of the free people of color appeared in parade dress and quietly observed the proceedings.[6]

Although there were no serious disturbances, the free people of color continued to be a source of anxiety among those whites who feared another Haitian revolution. Claiborne tried desperately to prevent the immigration of West Indian blacks, but he was largely unsuccessful. The resident free people of color successfully hid and protected the newcomers.[7]

The existence of the militia of free men of color was an extremely delicate matter. The governor thought that recommissioning the corps would be an insult to those slave-holding states in which there was opposition to such recognition of nonwhite people, and in which the fear of armed blacks was a constant bogey. Also, federal law permitted service only to whites. Claiborne knew, however, that the free people of color jealously guarded the privilege of performing military service as some recognition of their superiority over slaves and as a basis for claiming citizenship status. To disband the corps would create a large faction of discontented persons and would require some means of confiscating their weapons. Therefore, he deferred any decision until he received orders from his superiors.[8]

Meantime, in January of 1804, the free persons of color presented a petition to Claiborne, offering their services to the American government. Claiborne received instruction from the secretary of war, Henry Dearborn, suggesting that he continue the corps in a diminished fashion and, if possible, find some means of presenting them with a standard. Claiborne publicly presented the corps with a standard on January 21, 1804. At the same time, to prevent disorder, he presented new flags to white militia units.[9]

Claiborne's action temporarily satisfied the free people of color but brought forth roars of outrage from the whites.[10] When the legislature met to pass a general militia law in April of 1805, it restricted service to "all able-bodied white male citizens ages sixteen to fifty."[11] When free persons of color expressed their anger at this legislation, Claiborne reported to the War Department doubts concerning their dependability in case of danger. They saw the legislation as the beginning of a trend toward reducing them to near-slave status. The governor believed that "this neglect soured considerably their regard for the American Government."[12]

Claiborne continued his efforts to have the militia of free persons of color recognized by law during the next few years; but the white population, increasingly apprehensive, feared that a force of armed nonwhites might become the leaders of a slave insurrection. Meanwhile, the legislature passed stringent laws regulating free persons of color. One statute, adopted in 1806, made it a crime for a free person of color to insult, strike, or "presume to conceive themselves equal to white persons." Free persons of color were admonished never to speak to, nor to answer a white person except with respect; failure to do so would bring imprisonment according to the severity of the offense.[13] A statute passed in March of 1808 required the notation "free man" or "woman of color" to be placed after the name of such persons on all documents or legal papers, and in all notices. A fine of one hundred dollars was the penalty enacted for noncompliance.[14]

Claiborne's efforts to organize the increasing population of free persons of color into militia companies gained support when the free men of color helped to suppress a slave revolt in January of 1811. Additionally, in the summer of 1812, a new Spanish governor arrived at Pensacola with one hundred and fifty black troops among his forces, which directed attention to the desirability of using this largely untapped source of manpower.[15] Claiborne's continued efforts, coupled with the evidence of the Spanish attitude and the demonstrated loyalty of the free men of color during the slave revolt, led the first state legislature to permit the limited service of blacks in the militia. An act of September 1812 authorized the governor to organize companies of militia from among the "creoles" of color and those who paid a state tax. The commander, who was to be white, would choose the other officers. There would be four companies containing sixty-four men each, including officers. Membership in the corps was restricted to the owners, or sons of owners, of landed property worth three hundred dollars. These regulations were designed to include only those free people of color who had the greatest stake in the continued existence of the society as it was.[16] Benefiting from the chaotic conditions, the free persons of color had maintained successfully their status as slightly higher than that of slaves. In contrast, at this time, nonwhites of all classes were completely excluded by law from armed service in the militia of all other states.

The federal government made no effort to change the militia law to permit the general use of blacks during the War of 1812. The Militia Act of 1792 remained operative throughout this whole period. The act of 1790, providing for a regular army of volunteers, was amended from time to time, but no mention of race or color was ever included in it. The acts of March 3, 1794, March 16, 1802, December 24, 1811, January 11, 1812, January 20, 1813, and January 27, 1814, all provided for the enlistment of any effective able-bodied man into the national army. Yet, despite the burning of Washington, the severe military campaigns of 1814 and the prospect of worse ones in 1815, and the difficulty of providing sufficient manpower, the government did not enlist blacks generally or conscript white men.[17]

When Congress met in September of 1814, the military forces of the United States consisted of 62,448 men. Bounties of a half-section of land, a cash payment of $124, and a monthly wage of $8 plus clothing were not sufficient inducements to obtain the necessary number of volunteers. Congress, soberly, listened to President Madison explain that it must consider the eventuality of a British victory in the next year or provide more effectively for the national defense.[18]

Madison's secretary of war, James Monroe, asked Congress for the creation of a permanent national military force of forty thousand additional men. Monroe explained that even though public opinion was opposed to a standing army, a large permanent force was necessary. He proposed that all free men between the ages of eighteen and forty-five should be formed into classes. Each class would be required to furnish a quota of men for the regular army to serve for the duration of the war. If any class failed to furnish its quota, the required number of men would be drafted. The draftee must serve or provide a substitute. Draftees would receive the same bounties as regular volunteers. Monroe was certain of the constitutionality of his proposal, since Congress had the power to raise and support armies. This power was unqualified, and therefore, the means necessary to carry it into effect was automatically given. Monroe further contended that the law of self-preservation gave the nation a right to call upon its manhood to repel invasions. The militia laws of the various states compelled service of all able-bodied white males and exacted penalties for delinquency. If the states could compel citizens to serve in their defense, he believed, the national government could do likewise.[19]

Monroe's proposals were strongly supported by the Republicans, on the basis of expediency, and clamorously opposed by Federalists, who found themselves uncomfortably arguing on the basis of states's rights. In spite of the Federalist objections that the bill gave unconstitutional powers to the national government, that conscription was a tyrannical policy the people would never accept, and that the rich would escape service by buying substitutes, the bill was passed by the Senate on November 22, 1814.[20]

The bill was sent to the House, where the Republicans were in the majority and where George M. Troup, Republican of Georgia, was chairman of the Military Affairs Committee. The committee had already been considering Monroe's proposals and had prepared its own bill on the subject. When the militia bills were brought before the House for full debate, battle lines were drawn exactly as they were in the Senate. The Federalists, even such "Nationalists" as Daniel Webster, opposed the bill, largely using states' rights arguments, while such states' righters as John C. Calhoun upheld the bill from the "Nationalist" point of view. This disposition of forces was due to Federalist opposition to the war itself and the economic disorganization existing in New England. Calhoun and the "Warhawks," on the other hand, strongly favored the prosecution of the war. The House finally passed the bill by an almost straight party vote of seventy-seven Republicans plus only two Federalists. However, fifty-one Federalists and twenty Republicans voted no.[21]

The bill went back to the Senate on December 15 for concurrence and then to a joint conference committee for approval. Public debate, becoming increasingly shrill, partially prompted the calling of the Hartford Convention, which brought together the objectors to the whole war policy of the Madison administration.[22]

In the conference committee the conscription bill was bitterly contested. It became increasingly evident that the legislators were terrified by the display of public sentiment against the bill, and some means of disposing of it entirely had to be found. Finally, on December 28, Rufus King, a Federalist senator from New York, introduced a motion to postpone discussion until the second Monday in March, which was the day after the expiration of the Thirteenth Congress. Everyone knew that passage of the motion meant the rejection of the whole bill. The motion carried, killing the first proposal for national conscription. Although the passage of the conscription bill would not have meant the immediate eligibility of free blacks for service in the militia, since it specifically referred only to free white males, in the debate there was some indication that the adoption of conscription would have forced the issue. Repeating arguments similar to those made in the Constitutional Convention, some Northern senators thought it unfair that under the Three-Fifths Clause blacks were represented in the Congress but did not have to serve in the militia. If quotas were assigned, they should be based strictly on total population. Southern senators objected that this would mean higher quotas for their states to fill since they would not arm the blacks and only white men could be used to fill them.[23]

Although the national government still did not permit the service of blacks in the national militia, Governor Claiborne completed the organization of the free militia of color in Louisiana just in time for the War of 1812. In December of 1813, the president of the United States requisitioned troops from the state militias to continue the prosecution of the war. Governor Claiborne immediately ordered militia companies throughout the state to form and assemble at New Orleans. The response was good from the rural areas, but there was a great deal of opposition in the city. The inhabitants feared that the militia would march off and leave them undefended against a possible invasion. Claiborne was forced to discharge all militia units and deny the federal request. In the summer of 1814, New

Orleans was disturbed by increasing rumors of an approaching British expeditionary force. Large numbers of men gladly formed militia companies and willingly performed daily drill. The free population of color asked for permission to increase the size of their militia corps. Undaunted by the impending danger, the white citizenry continued their objections to arming large numbers of nonwhites, who might be inflated by a sense of their own importance and begin demanding equal status with white persons. Claiborne thought that increasing the size of the corps of men of color would be militarily expedient, but he did not want to act in view of the objections of the white populace. He referred the matter to General Andrew Jackson, commanding the Seventh Military District, which included Louisiana, for his resolution.[24]

Jackson, engaged in strengthening the defenses of Mobile before moving to New Orleans, ordered Claiborne to assemble the entire state militia and muster it into the service of the United States. Upon receiving reports of increasingly disloyal sentiment among the free people of color, Jackson issued a proclamation praising them for their long military tradition, commending their offer to serve against the British, and promising them an opportunity to serve on a plane of equality with white soldiers.[25] As soon as Jackson's proclamation was published, a committee of white persons called on Claiborne to protest this recognition of the free people of color.[26] Claiborne reported their protests to Jackson, but the general did not seem alarmed. He was more concerned about dissipating possible subversion in a time of crisis. He commented that if the free men of color demonstrated merit they could be used against the enemy, and if they demonstrated disloyalty, they could be moved to the rear where they could do no harm.[27] Although Jackson's acceptance of the free volunteers of color could have been rationalized legally within the regular army statute (which had no racial clause), within American legal tradition, compelling military necessity justified their use.

Jackson finally left the defenses of Mobile in November, arriving in New Orleans on December 1 to take personal charge of military affairs there. He found Claiborne and the legislature at odds over necessary provisions for defense. The legislators had approved a twenty-thousand dollar loan for fortifications, they had asked each citizen who owned more than one gun to donate one to the common defense, and they had appropriated eleven thousand dollars to Jackson for military purposes. Claiborne believed that these measures were inadequate.[28] As soon as he arrived in New Orleans, Jackson discussed defenses with Claiborne and the legislature and arranged for meetings with officers of various militia units. When the officers of the battalion of free men of color called on him, he again commended their loyalty and apparent willingness to fight.[29]

Jean Baptiste Savary, a free man of color and Dominican refugee who had been an officer in the French army, offered to form a battalion from among the Dominican immigrants of color in New Orleans. Jackson accepted the offer and appointed Savary as one of the captains in the unit. The free men of color were formed into two battalions, with Michael Fortier, who was white, commanding the entire corps. Jean Daquin, a white Dominican refugee, was made commander of the Dominican battalion, and Pierre Lacoste, a New Orleans planter, was named commander of the original battalion. Four hundred and thirty free men of color enrolled in the corps.[30]

The free men of color performed loyally in the ensuing battle with the British and won praises from all sides once the victory was won. Jackson issued a general order lauding their courage and perseverance. The state legislature passed resolutions congratulating the men and officers, along with the free women of color who served as nurses for those who were injured in the fighting.[31]

During the lull of peacetime, the faithful service of the free men of color did little to repel efforts to push the status of free persons closer and closer to that of slaves. The veterans were not invited to participate in the ceremonies held each year to commemorate the Battle of New Orleans. However, the state legislature did allocate pensions equal to those given white veterans to free men of color who were wounded in action. The pension for a private was eight dollars a month; that of Joseph Savary, former captain of the Dominican regiment, was thirty dollars a month.[32]

In January 1851 the veterans who were free men of color were asked to participate in the commemorative ceremonies. They were also present at the public presentation of an equestrian statue of Andrew Jackson in January 1856. Governor Henry Palfrey saw fit to entertain the group at dinner at his home on January 8, 1859, when he made a stirring speech about the continued loyalty of the free people of color to the ideals and traditions of the South. In the tension-filled years before the Civil War, it was considered wise to wax sentimental about the loyalty and valor of this important sector of the population.[33]

Because there was still no racial restriction placed on the enlistment of volunteers in the regular army, a few blacks other than the free men of color in New Orleans aided the American effort during the War of 1812. On October 24, 1814, the legislature of New York passed an act which provided for the enlistment of two regiments of free black volunteers for three years or the duration of the war. Slaves could be enlisted with the consent of their owners. The troops were guaranteed the same pay and allowances as other troops in the regular army. They were not a part of the state militia but would be ordered into active duty in the national army "in lieu of equal number of militia whenever the state militia is called." The New York proposal met with considerable approbation and some criticism. A correspondent to the *Daily National Intelligencer* from South Carolina thought that using blacks in the service was an ingenious means of "draining off free blacks." If they were in the army they could provide manpower, and many would be destroyed as casualties of war; many others would form attachments to other places "where they might remain after the war." An Ohioan wrote that he thought "in the present crisis a widespread use of blacks should be undertaken," but he was sure it would not be, "because of prejudice."[34] At the end of the War of 1812 a group of black veterans applied for bounty and land grants which were authorized for all volunteers and were sustained in their claims by the United States attorney general's office. William Wirt, who was attorney general at the time, explained that since there were no racial clauses in the regular army statutes, the service of blacks was legal and proper. There was no reason to deny them the same bounty and allowances given to other volunteers. However, he asserted his belief that Congress had not really intended to incorporate blacks into the army any more than in the militia. The army reinforced this interpretation by issuing a general order in February 1820 specifying that blacks would not be received in the regular army.[35]

The military statutes did not become an object of extended debate on the race question again until 1842, when John Calhoun of South Carolina asked in the Senate whether the absence of a racial clause in the army, navy, and Marine Corps statutes indicated an intention to enlist blacks. He was interested particularly in the Naval Service, where black sailors had been enlisted when necessary since the Revolution. Senator Richard H. Bayard of Delaware, who was chairman of the committee that presented the bill to the Senate, responded in the negative. The bill "left the laws in that respect as they now stood—that is, left the discretion to the proper Department." He presumed that "the Government was not going to order the enlistment of Negroes." Calhoun insisted that some racial clause should be put in to avoid incidents such as governmental refusal to permit black sailors to land in Southern ports, by limiting the service of blacks in some way. Furthermore he believed "it was wrong to bring those who have to sustain the honor and glory of the country down to a footing of the Negro race—to be degraded by being mingled and mixed up with that race." Bayard asserted that any particular problems that resulted from the service of blacks could be regulated by the department involved. Blacks had served in the Revolution, and he was not, therefore, "disposed to introduce an exception which would deprive the Government of the service of these men, if it should be deemed hereafter necessary." After Calhoun argued further that respect for the South and for white sailors ought to mean exclusion of blacks from the navy, Senator Benjamin Tappan of Ohio commented that he "was not aware that the employment of Negroes in public service had ever proved injurious to it. Then why not leave the matter as it had stood heretofore?" Officers should have the discretion to use blacks if necessary. Senator Samuel Phelps of Vermont agreed, pointing out that blacks had served also in the War of 1812. Of course everyone preferred to use white men, but not enough willing white men could always be found. Senator Thomas Hart Benton of Missouri thundered that "arms whether on land or water ought to be borne by the white race only." This was the first time he had heard that the black race was permitted under some circumstances to serve in the military forces. He, like Calhoun, was opposed to it. Senators Richard Young of Illinois and Perry Smith of Connecticut agreed with Phelps and Tappan, Smith pointing out the valuable service of the Rhode Island black regiment during the Revolutionary War. Senator Arthur Bagby of Alabama thought the discussion was improper. "The South has now to resort to prohibitory means to keep arms out of their hands, and to prevent their acquiring a knowledge of the use of them; but here it is proposed to receive them into the service and to train them to the use of arms." If military defense was necessary it should be done exclusively by white men. He was opposed "to the employment of the Negro race in any situation where it was necessary to put arms in their hands. Our [the South's] security forbids it." Levi Woodbury of New Hampshire tried to pacify the Southerners by asserting that even in the North blacks were forbidden militia service but that "in time of war, when all the great foundations of society are in jeopardy, war makes its own rules as it did in the Revolution." However, the Senate voted twenty-four to sixteen to insert a white-only clause in the marine and navy statutes and passed another measure introduced by William C. Preston of South Carolina to insert the same clause in the regular army statute. Although the bill passed, it was late in the session, and the House took no action on the measures. The sixteen who voted in opposition to the racial clause were Northerners.[36]

Because the supply of volunteers was more than adequate, there was no need during the Mexican war to enact a conscription law or to amend the militia law to include blacks. The congressional act providing for the prosecution of the war with Mexico authorized the president to employ the militia, the regular army and navy, and as many as fifty thousand volunteers. Jordan Noble, a veteran of the Battle of New Orleans, was among a small group of blacks who claimed service in the Mexican War. The court-martial records of a few black offenders clearly indicate that there were at least some black volunteers who served in the army. It seems, however, that the number of blacks who were accepted for the service was rather small and insignificant even when compared with the number who fought in the War of 1812.[37]

In the 1840's and 1850's, as antislavery sentiment intensified, the issue of black militia service was increasingly discussed. At conventions of free blacks in New York in 1845, in Troy in 1847, and in Cleveland, the issue of militia service was discussed; Henry Highland Garnet's position that inclusion in the militia as a right and duty of citizenship should be required of free blacks was adopted in 1853. Blacks in Massachusetts petitioned the state legislature, unsuccessfully, to enact a law permitting their enlistment in the regular militia or to establish a black militia company, since an Irish company had been recently approved. The subject was aired thoroughly at the Massachusetts Constitutional Convention that year. A petition was offered by John P. Coburn and others that the color distinction should be removed from the militia provisions. There was a long debate on the rights of blacks in which Henry Wilson of Natick asked whether the governor could serve as commander of the militia if he were black. (Blacks were permitted to vote and hold political office in Massachusetts.) Abbot of Lowell responded in the negative but explained that the governor could appoint someone else. Rufus Choate, the state attorney general, reminded the delegates that they could not raise a black regiment or enlist black men in the militia so long as the federal statute remained unrepealed. Still Wilson suggested that a voluntary organization of black men could be recognized by the state under a provision declaring that they were not part of the militia. Since it was generally concluded that this would be a transparent effort to evade federal law, that suggestion was rejected by a vote of 78 to 112.[38]

Again, in the Massachusetts legislature in 1860, the issue was the subject of heated debate. Blacks petitioned the legislature to remove the word *white* from the state militia law. William Whiting, who was representing Plymouth in the Senate, favored the motion to take the provision out of the state statute because he believed the argument that the state militia was not militia of the United States could be won. He wanted to reinterpret the power of Congress to organize the militia to permit states to enlist whomever they pleased. When the state militia was called into active national service, only then would the national laws category restricting service to white males apply. His support was based "also on the claims the colored people have on the government on the grounds of past militia service both in the revolution and the War of 1812." He thought these precedents, although not technically legal and occurring during actual wartime necessity, might be stretched to provide a rationale for peacetime militia service of some kind. The bill was assigned to a third reading by a vote of twenty-four to eight. Supporters of Governor Nathaniel Banks argued that the bill should not be passed, because it would place the governor in the position of having to veto a controversial bill on the grounds of constitutionality. As Warren Ordway of Bradford, who voted against the bill, explained it, Banks's Democratic presidential nomination hinged on the outcome. If they passed the bill and he vetoed it as illegal, this would stir up anti-slavery supporters. In the House, Amos Merrill of Boston responded that he was not impressed with this argument, and he thought the white-only clause should be removed because "it helps to continue the degradation of the black race which is the basis of slavery itself." Moses Kimball of Boston agreed that retaining the word *white* was "harboring an insidious distinction." But the bill failed of passage by a vote of seventy to eighty-six in the House. Whiting's desire to challenge the federal statute did not prevail. Massachusetts did not provide for the inclusion of blacks in the militia until the Civil War, when the national statute was changed.[39]

After the Revolutionary War, whatever liberal temper was generated by the revolt against the British was doused by a conservative reaction. Along with other movements for social progress, antislavery projects and efforts to enlarge the civil rights of free blacks were defeated. The use of black troops had not been absolutely necessary to the war effort, and no large-scale use of black soldiers occurred. The inclusion of a racial clause in the Militia Act of 1792 was to be expected. The omission of such a clause in the regular army act of 1790 occurred because, historically, regular armies could be augmented in the time of crisis by whatever manpower was available. The absence of a racial clause was not designed to encourage black enlistments but to permit them when absolutely necessary. The militia was a social and military organization in time of peace; in time of war, service in it was both a badge and responsibility of citizenship. State legislatures, following the example of the national government passed militia laws excluding blacks. Forced by consideration of the dangers involved in upsetting a tradition of militia duty by free people of color, in an atmosphere of crisis, only the Louisiana legislature provided for the continued existence of a militia corps of free men of color. Louisiana free Negroes saw extensive service during the War of 1812, and there were a few blacks in the army in other areas of the country. Louisiana free persons of color continued to enjoy more privileges under the law than free blacks elsewhere in the nation. During the Mexican War a few blacks joined volunteer army units, but their numbers were apparently neither large nor significant. In neither the War of 1812 nor the Mexican War did military necessity compel a thorough revision of the law of slavery and noncitizenship status of blacks.

## CHAPTER THREE

# NO BLACKS NEED APPLY

By the time of the Civil War, a sharpened distinction between militia and volunteer, or regular, military service was generally accepted in American law and society. Militia service as described in the 1792 statutes was required and permitted to white male citizens who provided their own arms and equipment. In 1808 Congress began to provide money to arm and equip the militia. Congress also provided from time to time for the recruitment of volunteer officers to be named by state governors. Service in the militia, largely a social organization, was a mark of citizenship, and its officer corps contained the most respectable people in the community. Men in the ordinary state militia were usually of modest means; those in voluntary militia companies were wealthier, as could be seen by their gaudy dress. In the South, militia titles were important, and were used in ordinary conversation. Gentlemen distinguished between the "trash," who were willing to serve as professionals in the regular army, especially in a country with as much opportunity as existed in the United States, and the honest yeomen in the militia. The trash in the army could be augmented by using blacks in time of crisis, since army service did not create a presumption of equality or citizenship status. Those were the long-standing attitudes toward military service when the Civil War began.[1]

When Fort Sumter was fired upon on April 12, 1861, the total strength of the Army of the United States was only 16,402. This included officers and men, present and absent, scattered throughout the country, North and South, East and West. According to the census of 1860, the total population of the states and territories was 31,433,321; of these there were 5,624,065 white males between the ages of eighteen and forty-five. The nineteen states which remained faithful to the Union had a white population of 18,936,579, as compared with 5,499,467 white inhabitants in the eleven states which seceded. The four border states—Kentucky, Maryland, Missouri, and Delaware—had a total white population of 2,589,533, from which both sides drew manpower during the war. There were some 3,953,760 slaves and 488,070 free people of color in all the states and territories at the time. Of the total number of slaves, the Confederate states contained 3,521,111. The four border states had 429,401.[2] Legally, all of the able-bodied male citizens between the ages of eighteen and forty were militiamen and could be called forth to suppress insurrections. In the North, most of these potential militiamen were unorganized and without the least semblance of training. Black males, slave and free, had been generally excluded from consideration for militia service since the act of 1792. The usual legal condition of blacks was still slavery and noncitizenship, and this had been reaffirmed recently by the Supreme Court in the *Dred Scott* case. Since the establishment of the Republic, neither humanitarian concern, spiritual striving, political considerations, fear of slave insurrections, nor varying degrees of military necessity had compelled significant alteration in the legal status of blacks.[3]

Three days after the firing at Fort Sumter President Lincoln called 75,000 militiamen from the states into national service for three months in order to inflate the puny military forces of the United States and to put down the rebellion. The immediate response was heartening. A total of 91,816 men responded to the first call. On May 3 the president, without congressional legislation, issued a proclamation increasing the size of the regular army to 39,973, but few men were obtained for the regular service. The idea of enlistment for a long term in the regular army had little appeal. The president asked for volunteers to increase the size of the navy, and again the number who volunteered surpassed the number requested.[4]

The first Battle of Bull Run (July 20-23, 1861) demonstrated the ineffectiveness of hastily drawn, inadequately trained volunteers. In the midst of Bull Run, Congress authorized the induction of 500,000 state militiamen for service of at least six months but no more than three years. In the first days of battle, little encouragement was needed as men flocked to the national colors. The number of men furnished by the states under these first calls totaled 700,680. The government lacked facilities for supply and training on such a large scale, and on December 3, 1861, the secretary of war began discouraging the acceptance of volunteers unless they were specifically requisitioned by his department.[5]

In the first months of the war many blacks, believing the war could be made into a war to free the slaves, were as eager to join the service as their white compatriots, but the government did not yet find it necessary to accept them. The law still restricted militia duty to white males only, and the regular army still did not enlist blacks. Although blacks and abolitionists from the beginning regarded the war as leading to abolition, the majority of whites did not. Frederick Douglass might sense clearly that "once they let the black man get upon his person the brass letters U.S.; let him get an eagle on his button and a musket on his shoulder and bullets in his pocket, and there is no power on earth which can deny that he has earned the right to citizenship in the United States," but that was not the rule in the *Dred Scott* case or the will of the 1861 majority. Groups of blacks asked the War Department to enlist them in the army, but they were refused. The regular army statutes permitted black enlistments, but War Department policy had long been black exclusion unless there was some overwhelming necessity. There did not seem to be a pressing need for extra manpower, and there was a concerted effort to maintain the loyalty of the border slave states, which might be stampeded into secession by propositions to arm blacks. There were many others who feared any policy that would bring an influx of freed blacks to the North and create a difficult Northern problem of race adjustment and assimilation. In the early months of the war, the newspapers constantly enunciated the general feeling that the war was being waged to save the Union and that schemes to free blacks or arm blacks or in any way to alter the status of blacks had no place in the struggle. As one newspaper put it, "slavery is merely the existing, not the ultimate, cause which has produced secession. A National Bank, under some circumstances might have proved an exciting cause to produce the same effect. . . ." Furthermore, the issue is to save the Union and it is "precisely what it would be if there was not a Negro slave on American soil." Meanwhile, Northern newspapers continually discounted rumors that black regiments were being raised by the South just as Southern newspapers excited local sentiments with reports that free blacks in the North were being armed to be sent to start slave revolts.[6]

Despite the public discussion, the policy of the Lincoln administration in 1861 remained clear—no blacks to be armed, all fugitive slaves to be returned to their masters. The War Department ordered Union generals not to interfere with slavery where they found it and to suppress all slave insurrections. When John C. Fremont, in August of 1861, proclaimed all slaves or rebels in the Department of Missouri forever free, Lincoln was quick to disavow this action and forced the withdrawal of the proclamation. He modified Fremont's action by asserting that the policy of the Confiscation Act of 1861 was that slaves actually used by the rebels could be freed. Lincoln wanted to make it clear that he was not proposing general abolition.[7]

While the North maintained a policy of exclusion, some Southern states passed legislation to renew a practice which had developed during the colonial period. On June 28, 1861, the Tennessee Legislature authorized the drafting of free blacks along with white males. The statute indicated that the blacks would be required to perform fatigue duty and menial services for the white militiamen. They would be paid eight dollars a month and one ration a day. The South Carolina legislature passed a similar statute in order to utilize blacks in the war effort. In Louisiana, matters advanced much more rapidly. On April 23, 1861, a New Orleans paper noted meetings of free men of color called to discuss possible participation in the war. The article closed with the observation that "these men whose ancestors distinguished themselves at the battle of New Orleans are determined to give new evidences of their bravery." On April 27, the same newspaper carried an advertisement by Jordan Noble, drummer boy at Chalmette in 1815, asking all free persons of color who wished to offer their services to the Confederate government as Home Guards to attend a meeting at five o'clock that evening. Three days later the *New Orleans True Delta* reported that Governor Thomas Moore was thinking of organizing free men of color into a regiment. Such a regiment would teach the "Black Republicans of the North that they [blacks] knew their false from their true friends." On May 1, the free nurses of color of the city, organized since the War of 1812, offered their service to the Confederacy in case of attack. Their offer was accepted by Major John T. Monroe, who praised their sense of duty and loyalty to the Confederate cause. On May 12, 1861, Governor Moore issued a proclamation providing for the enrollment of free men of color to form a regiment, with officers chosen from among them, to protect New Orleans in case of Union attack. The regiment was designated the First Native Guards, Louisiana Militia, Confederate States of America. By the end of May, a regiment containing 440 men and officers had been formed.[8] Negroes were also recruited for militia units in other areas of the state, so that by early 1862, there were more than 3,000 members of black military organizations in Louisiana. This was a substantial figure, since the entire free Negro population of the state in 1860 was only 18,547, of whom nearly 11,000 lived in New Orleans.

While Louisiana prepared to use her free men of color as soldiers, the Union remained uncommitted. Simeon Cameron, the Secretary of War, made some efforts to provide for the use of blacks in the Union army, but these attempts were met with disapproval and, in some degree, hastened the end of his ill-starred career. Since more and more blacks drifted into camp wherever the army could be found, Union generals out in the field were forced to make practical decisions regarding their disposition. General Benjamin Butler's policy, adopted at Fortress Monroe in the spring of 1861, of using black "contrabands" as cooks, teamsters, and laborers, was largely followed. Butler decided that since the South regarded blacks as property, they, like all other property of the enemy captured or abandoned in wartime, could by used by the victors. Butler's policy was in part legislated by Congress in the Confiscation Act of August 1861. The act declared that property, including slaves, used by the Confederates in aid of the rebellion was lawfully subject to capture by the Union forces. Slaves used by the rebels were to be set free. General Charles Halleck, in command at St. Louis, adopted a policy quite different from Butler's. On November 30, he issued his controversial General Order Number Three, remanding all fugitive slaves from Union lines and directing that they be sent back to their masters. They would not be permitted to encumber the army. Halleck justified his order on the basis of reported instances of spying by fugitives, who gave information on Union troop movements to the rebels.[9]

On December 31, 1861, when the Thirty-Seventh Congress convened and concern and confusion over the disposition of fugitive and abandoned slaves was quite evident, a spate of bills was introduced on the subject. Lyman Trumbull, a representative from Illinois, introduced a measure which would confiscate the slaves of rebels, whether these slaves were used to aid the rebellion or not. His bill was tabled. Owen Lovejoy, another representative from Illinois, proposed that the return of fugitive slaves be made a penal offense and that Halleck's General Order Number Three be revoked. In the Senate, Henry Wilson and Charles Sumner offered legislation for similar purposes. These proposals were considered, but no legislation was passed on the subject.[10] The majority of Congress did not yet find it necessary to recognize abolition and emancipation as war aims.

Congress made little effort to encourage the general enlistment of blacks into the service; the rush of white volunteers still made consideration of the subject nonessential. By February 1862, however, the War Department began to doubt the wisdom of its December policy of discouraging volunteers. Edwin Stanton, the new Secretary of War, issued an executive order on February 14, which expressed his concern over the continued availability of manpower to satisfy Union needs. It seems that the military reverses suffered by the newly levied and poorly trained forces "discouraged the loyal and gave new hope to the insurgents." Voluntary enlistments fell off and desertions became increasingly evident. There was some speculation that conscription might become necessary. Despite Stanton's fears, the administration apparently concluded that the Army of 637,126 men was sufficient. On April 3, 1862, the War Department issued a general order stopping all recruitment for the Army and closing the recruiting stations. Although subsequent events proved the action ill-advised, Congress and the people deemed it necessary to stop the enormous expenditures involved in recruiting, and the department yielded to popular demand.[11]

The Lincoln administration acted in the face of the pressure of public opinion and the difficulties involved in feeding, clothing, housing, and arming large numbers of volunteers when sufficient numbers seemed to have already been taken into service.

Meanwhile, the Confederate Congress had provided Jefferson Davis with the power to raise a long-term army which could be numerically superior to that at the disposal of President Lincoln on a short-term basis. Prior to the bombing of Fort Sumter, the Confederate Congress had authorized Davis to raise an army of 100,000 men. Furthermore, the Confederate president had issued a call for 32,000 men immediately after the war began. A law of May 8, 1861, delegated to Davis broad powers to accept volunteers without regard to apportionment among the states. He was also given the sole right to confer commissions and was relieved from the necessity of issuing formal calls for troops. A law passed in December 1861 made the term of enlistment three years instead of one and fixed the bounty for volunteers at fifty dollars. On April 16, 1862, while Stanton was ordering the close of recruitment offices at the North, the Confederate Congress passed an act which subjected all able-bodied white men between the ages of eighteen and thirty-five to compulsory military service and renewed the enlistment of men already in the army. Thus, all effective white males were required to serve for the duration of the war. Also, in early 1861, some of the Confederate states had already organized free men of color and were preparing to use them in the war effort.[12]

During the months of April and May, while recruitment was halted in the North, sentiment increased in favor of enlisting blacks in the Union Army. Some Northern newspapers expressed the view that since blacks could better withstand the Southern climate, they should be used as extensively as possible. In November 1861 the first experimental use of blacks occurred in the Department of the South, when the expedition of Admiral Samuel Dupont and General William T. Sherman captured the Sea Islands off South Carolina. General Sherman had been authorized to use fugitive slaves in whatever way he deemed beneficial to the service. Sherman did not arm the slaves but put them to work, under the direction of the Treasury Department, cultivating cotton on the abandoned plantations. The Treasury Department appointed Edward L. Pierce to supervise the project. Pierce, a Boston lawyer and abolitionist, recruited New England teachers to come to Beaufort and attempt to uplift and educate the black slaves.[13]

When General David Hunter succeeded Sherman in March 1862, he found the military force available in South Carolina insufficient for the maintenance of his position. Therefore, he decided to employ the large numbers of local blacks militarily. On April 13, 1862, Hunter issued a proclamation declaring that all slaves of rebels in the Department of the

South were confiscated and freed. He based this order on the provisions of the First Confiscation Act of August 1861. On May 9 he issued another, more broadly-based proclamation declaring that the states of Georgia, South Carolina, and Florida were under martial law. Under martial law the military commander had the power to take whatever action was necessary to preserve the army and society in order to advance the war effort. Since maintaining slavery was incompatible with the army's puposes, Hunter reasoned that the necessity for martial law was a basis for declaring all slaves forever free. When President Lincoln learned of Hunter's order he issued a proclamation of his own, denouncing it as illegal and unauthorized. Lincoln declared that neither General Hunter nor anyone else had been given permission to make proclamations concerning the freedom of slaves.[14] The administration was still not ready, by altering the status of blacks, to disaffect the border slave states; furthermore, Lincoln did not want to alienate those Unionists who were not interested in abolition. On April 10, Congress had passed Lincoln's proposal providing that "primary aid" would be given to any of the border slave states if they adopted emancipation; and on April 12, Congress had enacted compensated emancipation in the District of Columbia, but the border slave state officials remained opposed generally to relinquishing their slaves. Colonization outside the United States suggested by Lincoln in mid-1862 as a solution for the problem of what to do with the blacks ultimately also seemed impractical and impossible to achieve.

In spite of Lincoln's disapproval, General Hunter went forward with his plans for recruiting slaves. He issued orders to bring all able-bodied blacks into camp at Hilton Head, where they were impressed into his First South Carolina Colored Regiment. Some of the blacks came willingly, but many were forcibly inducted into the service. When newspaper correspondents got wind of Hunter's experiment, the press was filled with arguments concerning the desirability of arming blacks. Many newspapers expressed great concern over the possibility of blacks becoming officers. No white citizen of the country could be expected to serve under a black commander. The *Boston Journal* was sorely tried over the matter of conscripting blacks. All Union men enlisted heretofore had been volunteers, and it was generally held that conscripts were worse than convicts. Only the rebels resorted to conscription. Congress eventually took notice of Hunter's project. On June 9, 1862, Charles Wickliffe of Kentucky instigated the passage of a House resolution instructing the War Department to provide information concerning Hunter's activities. Stanton replied that his department had not authorized the recruitment and arming of blacks and ordered Hunter to reply to the House. Hunter, in a rather sharply worded letter to the House of Representatives, pointed to Simeon Cameron's authorization to General Sherman in October of 1861 as the basis of his recruiting activities. Cameron had authorized Sherman to use blacks in whatever way he considered necessary, but Sherman never attempted to arm blacks. Cameron was, of course, no longer in the War Department, and Hunter was not Sherman.[15]

The recruitment offices in the North remained closed from December 31, 1861, to June 6, 1862. Hunter's efforts to recruit blacks began during this lull, which was created by a false sense of security in the ability of the North to suppress the rebellion in a matter of months. Hunter and the other generals in the field were, in May, already feeling the inadequacy of their resources and the need for additional troops. After the disastrous results of the Peninsular Campaign and the increasing losses of manpower due to sickness, desertion, and battle losses, the War Department ordered the reopening of recruitment offices in June.[16]

Despite the reopening of the recruitment offices, the enthusiastic response of white males in the first year was not repeated. The unfavorable outcomes of the Seven Days' Battle and McClellan's March on Richmond undoubtedly had a depressing effect on Northern sentiments and dampened the enthusiasm of prospective militiamen. On June 28, the governors of seventeen loyal states called on the president and requested him to ask the states for additional troops, which they would make every effort to provide. Lincoln responded with a call on July 2 for 300,000 additional three-year volunteers. Men came in so slowly that many thought the Union might have to resort to conscription. Secretary of State William Seward said that Congress was slowly beginning to realize the emergency and that a draft would in the long run prove indispensable, but the old way had to be tried first. The need to assure equal contributions of manpower was satisfied by assigning to each state quotas based on population. In the long run, the July 2 quotas were filled, but the slowness of the response was not only disheartening, it also portended a worse response in the future.[17]

The continuing military crisis led to congressional passage of the General Militia Act of July 17, 1862, and the Second Confiscation Act. The Militia Act included limited provisions for the use of persons of African descent in the militia for the first time. It empowered the president to call upon the states for 300,000 nine-months men. If for any reason the states failed to provide the men, the president was authorized to make all necessary rules and regulations to fill the quotas. The enrollment included all able-bodied male citizens between the ages of eighteen and forty-five, to be apportioned among the states on the basis of population. The act authorized the president to receive blacks into the service for fatigue duty or any other military or naval service for which they might be found competent. The act further empowered the president to emancipate any black soldiers who were enlisted and the families of such soldiers so long as their former masters were rebels. However, as a continuing indication of inferior status, the black soldiers would be paid three dollars a month less than white privates in the army. The Confiscation Act gave the president the power to employ persons of African descent as he needed to suppress the rebellion.

The passage of the 1862 Militia Act marked an extraordinary change in traditional military policy. Since the colonial period the distinction between militia duty as an indication of citizenship status and volunteer or regular army duty as the occupation of the dregs of humanity had stood the test of time and numerous crises. Now, necessity had become so compelling that even the Militia Act was changed. Militia would still be called from the states by the president, but the states would be able to use black men to fill their quotas if white men could not be obtained. Many governors were willing to provide militia but could not force the men to serve. Blacks who were available and who were willing to serve were an obvious militia resource. Much like the result of the crisis in England in the seventeenth century, when the manpower used for the militia became more like the regular army, necessity blurred the distinction between the militia and the regular army in the North. The call of July 17, 1862, was a last-ditch effort to make the militia system work by expanding it to permit the use of traditional "undesirable" blacks. Military necessity had compelled the Congress to make another attempt, within the framework of the generally understood tenets of federalism, to utilize state governments in furnishing the manpower required for war purposes. However, the change provided a legal basis for increasing claims to citizenship status by blacks.[18]

The Confiscation Act and the Militia Act were not passed in the Congress without difficulty. Generally, border state representatives opposed arming the slaves, freeing the families of slave soldiers if the masters were disloyal, and the confiscation of slaves of rebels. Arming slaves, it was argued by Willard Saulsbury of Delaware in the Senate and Charles Wickliffe of Kentucky in the House, would mean conceding that twenty million white men could not subdue the rebellion. Furthermore, slaves were unfit for service; no white men would serve with them; arming them might stimulate discussion of abolition, and interference with slave property was a violation of states' rights. Those who favored the acts providing for the legal use of black soldiers argued that manpower needs, the precedent established during the Revolutionary War, and the sickly conditions of white men exposed to the Southern climates dictated the use of black soldiers. Advocates such as James Lane of Kansas, Jacob Howard of Michigan, Preston King of New York, Timothy O. Howe of Wisconsin, and James A. Harlan of Iowa, in the Senate, and William Kelley of Pennsylvania, William Windom of Minnesota, and William Lansing of New York, in the House, focused on the ultimate effects of the bill in the congressional debates. On July 11, 1862, Howe pointed to the recent defeats of the Union Army "down on the James River" in the Seven Days' Battle as a reason for providing more manpower by passing the bill. King, too, referred to "the mangled corpses of thousands of our young men sunk in the marshes of the Chickahominy and other localities in the Southern States . . . as a reason why white men should be relieved from the diseases and death which have fallen upon them" by the use of black soldiers. Lane of Kansas forthrightly decided to "speak plainly" and face the issue of the long-range consequences of arming blacks. "After these men are armed they cannot be reenslaved. Rome knew that; our fathers in the Revolution knew that; our fathers in the War of 1812 knew that. . . ." He was correct, since slaves who served in the patrol army during the Revolution were manumitted, and among the reasons for opposition to a policy of enlisting blacks offered by opponents was the necessity for emancipation or some improvement in legal status. Harlan, with whom Howard agreed, supported Lane's view. Harlan did "not remember a single example since civilization commenced, when slaves have been mustered into the armed services of a country and again attempted to be returned to slavery." Windom, Kelley, and Lansing, in the House, agreed that the reason why the services of slaves were needed was to resist " the wicked schemes of their masters." Opponents of the legislation agreed with John S. Phelps of Missouri that the fate of the freed slaves ought to be considered before the adoption of a military enlistment policy. Phelps pointed out that since some states in the North forbade the entry of free blacks, and Southern states generally required that freed blacks leave their borders, difficulties concerning their legal status would ensue. Although unresolved, the issue had been laid forthrightly before the Congress; arming the blacks under the Militia Act, when traditionally only citizens served in the militia, could mean taking a giant step along the road away from *Dred Scott* and toward abolition and citizenship status. But in 1862, military manpower needs, not a decision concerning the ultimate consequences of military policy, was uppermost in the words and votes of the majority of both Houses.[19]

Still mindful of tensions in the border slave states, instead of moving to arm blacks under the new law, on August 4, 1862, President Lincoln issued a call for 300,000 nine-months militia and ordered that states failing to furnish their quotas under the July 2 call should make up the deficiencies by August 15. The War Department regarded this as a necessary step taken by the government toward carrying out a settled principle upon which orderly government depends—that every citizen owes his country military service. The department issued detailed directions for the enrollment of the militia and for the draft in the states not furnishing their quotas of volunteers under the act of July 17, 1862. Governors were to appoint officials in each county who would make a roster of all men between the ages of eighteen and forty-five in their districts. A lottery would be held in which names would be picked from those on the roster, sufficient to fill the county's quota. A man whose name was drawn was required to report to the draft rendezvous within five days or furnish a substitute. The United States government paid the expenses incurred in the enrollment and draft and also appointed provost marshals in each state to enforce the induction of drafted men and to prevent desertions.[20]

The militia drafts were scheduled to begin on August 15, 1862, but were postponed because of delays in enrollment and apportionment, and the large numbers of requests for exemptions. The prospect of a draft instigated a great "skedaddle" of men who wanted to escape military service. On August 8, 1862, the State Department issued an order giving notice that no passports would be issued to men liable to the draft until their state quotas were filled. On August 13, 1862, Stanton issued orders severely restricting travel from state to state or even from district to district, hoping to squelch the draft dodgers. However, the draft was met almost everywhere with disfavor and was largely unsuccessful. The failure can be attributed to the natural disinclination of many Americans to be conscripts, the slowness of the enrollment procedure, the attractiveness of civilian employment and pursuits, the lack of energy on the part of some governors, and public dissatisfaction with their military leaders and the course of the war. The increasing prominence of abolition as a war aim also disenchanted many Unionists. Under the August 2 call, only 87,588 men were furnished, and of this number, many deserted before they could actually be inducted. Since a reliance upon the militia clause, which forced Congress to look to the states, had proved to be ineffective, many administrative leaders and some members of Congress now believed that state machinery could not be relied upon to furnish manpower for the war and that further legislation would have to be based on the power of Congress to raise and support armies.[21]

In the period between the failure of the militia drafts and the passage of the Conscription Act in March 1863, some resourceful, practical generals moved quickly to solve the manpower problem by recruiting fugitive slaves and free blacks. To Senator James Lane of Kansas, whose actions reflected his speeches in Congress, it was a matter of simple logic that in a war the opposing forces should use every resource available to them, and blacks were an obvious resource. It was a matter of utter indifference to him whether rebels were killed by white men or blacks, so long as they were killed. In August of 1862, Lane set up a recruiting office in Leavenworth and began openly enlisting white and black men. He kept the War

Department apprised of his efforts and informed Stanton that he was receiving blacks under the provisions of the Militia Act of July 17, 1862. Stanton delayed indicating his department's disapproval of Lane's activities until August 23, when he informed Lane that only the president could authorize the recruitment of blacks and that such regiments would not be accepted into the service. Lane continued to enroll blacks in spite of Stanton's reply. By October of 1862 Lane had his First Regiment of Kansas Colored volunteers filled and sent them on expeditions into Missouri.. The regiment continued its forays in Missouri and Arkansas and remained active in spite of the War Department's failure to muster them. In January of 1863, after a reversal in federal policy, the regiment was finally officially mustered in and served throughout the war.[22]

After Union soldiers entered New Orleans in May 1862, Benjamin Butler soon found that necessity compelled the use of black troops there. At first, Butler enforced prevailing Union policy by refusing to let fugitive slaves enter his lines. His willingness to revert from his earlier stance at Fortress Monroe occurred in part because unsanitary conditions and food shortages made sending slaves back to their masters seem reasonable. The army, under his orders, also enforced and even expanded many features of the antebellum slave codes. The pass system, now enforced against free blacks, and the imprisonment and flogging of recalcitrant slaves were allowed to continue. The exemption of Louisiana, because it was under Union control, from the Emancipation Proclamation, permitted the vestiges of slavery to wither away only gradually, even into the spring of 1863. Military necessity and the course of events slowly crumbled the last legal underpinnings of slavery.

At first, as elsewhere, even though many blacks, including the regiment organized by the Confederacy, offered their services to the Union Army, Butler refused to accept them. But his manpower problems made him change his mind, and by August 1862 he began the enlistment of blacks beginning with the Louisiana Native Guards, the regiment of free men of color organized by the Confederacy. The regiment organized by the Confederacy had not actually been used in warfare. Many of the men had volunteered because they felt they had no other choice. One free black declared in 1864 that free Negroes had contributed financially to the rebel cause and enlisted in the Confederate service, "but it is known to all under what pressure of public opinion, under what threats uttered by the promoters of secession this was done. . . ." According to Joseph T. Wilson in his *Black Phalanx*, the regiment was ordered to blow up the United States Mint in New Orleans when the Union army attacked the city, but refused to do so. Instead they had waited to see what would result from the Union victory.[23]

By November 24, 1862, Butler had organized three regiments and was still recruiting blacks. Although they were composed, in part, of free men of color, as the supplies of free blacks were exhausted, slaves were enlisted. Recruitment went forward rapidly and without difficulty. Some slaves saw the connection between the Union war effort and their freedom and rushed through Confederate pickets to join. Meetings were held where prominent free Negroes explained the benefits of Union service to the men. Julia LeGrand, a local resident, observed early in 1863 that blacks were "constantly singing 'Hang Jeff Davis on the Sour-Apple Tree.'" On February 21, 1863, when a crowd of whites was almost run down by a Union artillery battery, she declared, "the Negroes laughed and clapped their hands to see us run over and one screamed out, 'Here, let me get out of this d——d secesh.'" Blacks cheered Union troops as they marched throughout the city, and a number of the women presented flags to some of the regiments. Despite their wealth, jobs, and businesses, the free Negro officers, wrote R. H. Isabelle, one of their number, "all responded to the call of General Butler, closed up their establishments and enlisted in the Native Guards to fight for the Union." In a recruiting speech, P. B. S. Pinchback, who served as an officer in one of the regiments and was later lieutenant governor and governor of Louisiana during Reconstruction, expressed the late 1862 sentiments of many of the blacks. The men, he said, were being called upon to help free the oppressed and given an opportunity to enroll their names on the scroll of honor. The opportunity for service in the Union army was, he said:

The only time in my life I have felt anything like patriotism, my heart is full, my soul seams indeed in arms. . . . Oh, it is a Glorious sight to see those men that have bin raised under the yoke of slavery as they march out to drill[,] their heads erect, their Hartes beating high, their eyes Brightened, they feel the invigorating influence of breathing the Blessed air of Liberty. . . .

By promising the slaves their freedom, bounties and an opportunity to prove their manhood and to get revenge on their masters, the recruiters generated enthusiasm for service among the bondsmen. The provost marshal in one parish, Iberville, reported that the presence of recruiting officers had caused the blacks "to become excited and unmanageable"; whole plantations became deserted in one night. The provost marshal in Thibodaux asserted in November 1862 that "probably from 1,500 to 2,000 Negroes have been enlisted and run off to New Orleans." Butler reported his successful recruiting efforts to the War Department, but approval did not come immediately. Nonetheless, by the end of 1862, the manpower gap in Louisiana was being filled with black men in arms. Their recruitment and the necessity of continued use of large numbers of Louisiana blacks helped to eradicate the last vestiges of slavery under local law in Louisiana by the end of 1863. In October 1863 a state court ruled that blacks could no longer be held in slavery. On December 26, 1863, General Nathaniel Banks, who had replaced Butler as Union commander, ordered the removal of all signs in New Orleans regarding the sale and imprisonment of bondsmen. On January 11, 1864, he suspended all of the state's constitutional provisions regarding slavery.[24]

General Rufus Saxton, who was appointed military governor of the Sea Islands in July, was also faced with a critical manpower shortage. When he reported his difficulties to the War Department, despite the earlier refusal to ratify Lane, Hunter, and Butler's recruitment efforts, Stanton issued an order on August 25, 1862, authorizing the first official recruitment of blacks under the act of July 17, 1862. Stanton ordered Saxton to arm, uniform, and equip as many volunteers of African descent as he required not to exceed five thousand men. The order further stipulated that the men would receive the same pay and allowances as all other volunteers in the service. The July act had contemplated pay of three dollars less per month than the amount paid white privates for volunteers of African descent. Although he made clear his intention to use blacks only as laborers, the president was compelled to permit Stanton to issue these orders foreshadowing a very different policy. Despite the prejudices of white troops, jurisdictional difficulties with the new commanding general, Oliver M. Mitchel, and the bad effect of General Hunter's earlier effort, including the impressment of blacks into the army, Saxton succeeded in practically filling up his regiment. In November, the command was given to Thomas Wentworth Higginson, a Massachusetts abolitionist. Higginson was able to fill the ranks of the regiment by the end of the year. On January 31, 1863, it was mustered in as the fifth black regiment in the service.[25]

The early efforts to enroll and enlist blacks were largely motivated by practical considerations of manpower needs with a slight admixture of abolitionist sentiment. The inclusion of sections twelve, thirteen, and fourteen in the Militia Act of July 1862 permitting black enlistment was the obvious result of the efforts of abolitionists like Owen Lovejoy, Henry Wilson, and Charles Sumner, who also recognized Union manpower needs. They were aided by members of Congress like James Lane of Kansas, who were not necessarily interested in extinguishing slavery but favored using black manpower because it was needed. It was necessary to pass the Militia Act and Confiscation Acts of July 1862 to open service in the militia to blacks, to clarify the question of the status of fugitive slaves, and to legalize the use of slaves for ordinary service. The provision in the act that "persons of African descent" could be used put slaves of rebel masters in the South and in the border slave states in the same category as free blacks for the purpose of military service. Slaves of loyal masters were not enlisted under the provisions of the act. As a by-product of the black enlistment policy, the existence of slavery and the noncitizenship status of blacks were increasingly challenged. Some blacks and white abolitionists had regarded the war from the beginning as a vehicle for abolition and understood the concept that militia service was a badge of citizenship. The more winning the war and saving the Union came to require the use of black troops, the closer came abolition and the ultimate question of the extent of black citizenship status. One of the duties of able-bodied male citizens was to serve in the militia. Now, blacks could serve. The failure of the militia drafts in 1862 and the exigencies of battle paved the way for the adoption of national conscription. The adoption of national conscription would be another step toward black citizenship and civil rights protection.

## CHAPTER FOUR

# DRAFT RIOTS AND
# BLACK VOLUNTEERS

On January 1, 1863, after a series of Union defeats culminating at Fredericksburg on December 13, 1862, and the refusal of the border slave states to adopt his proposal for compensated emancipation, President Lincoln moved closer to an unqualified policy of arming blacks. The regular army statutes permitted the use of free black volunteers, and Congress had already authorized him to enlist persons of African descent including freedmen at his discretion in the militia. In the Emancipation Proclamation, the president indicated his intention to use blacks as "a fit and necessary war measure of suppressing the rebellion" but only in garrisons, forts, stations, and aboard naval vessels. As Lincoln took this halting step, the *New York Times* observed that increasing the military use of blacks would not only help the war effort but "since all nations have regarded this as the greatest or only claim to respect" it was a "noble and inspiring" opportunity to enhance the status of the race. Continuing battle losses gave clear indication that additional reliable sources of manpower would have to be found if the war was to be brought to a successful conclusion.[1]

Now to a public chorus of controversy over inflation, military reverses, and war was added the complaint that since the Emancipation Proclamation, the war had become a war to free the slaves and not to save the Union. Lincoln, attempting to decide whether and how to recruit large numbers of blacks, consulted a number of military-politicians including Daniel Ullmann, a New York lawyer and a Know-Nothing candidate for governor in 1856, who had commanded a New York regiment during the Peninsular Campaign in 1861. Based on his experience and knowledge, Ullmann urged Lincoln to arm as many blacks as possible. On January 13, Lincoln authorized Ullmann to raise four regiments of black volunteers, eventually designated the Corps d'Afrique, in the Louisiana area. Louisiana had 75,548 male slaves between the ages of eighteen and forty-five, according to the census of 1860. General Butler had already recruited large numbers of blacks to fill the ranks of his forces. It seemed obvious to Lincoln and Ullmann that Louisiana would be rich recruiting territory.[2]

Ullmann went to New York to gather white officers and to search for blacks who could read and write to serve as noncommissioned staff. Persons desiring commissions sought Ullmann out, but there was competition for the services of literate blacks. Other recruiters, allegedly agents of Governor John A. Andrew of Massachusetts, held mass meetings and offered second lieutenancies to qualified blacks. Ullmann was successful in enlisting a group of white officers and left for New Orleans in April. By May 19, 1863, Ullmann reported the successful recruitment of 1,976 "strong and intelligent" blacks.[3]

Meanwhile Congress was on the brink of passing a national draft act. Congressmen were involved in constant discussions of Union manpower needs and were well aware of the failure of the militia drafts initiated by the act of July 1862. They were also conscious of Lincoln's policy of gradualism concerning the arming of blacks in the light of continuing concern about the loyalty of slaveholders in the border states, although the Militia Act clearly gave him discretionary power. Neither President Lincoln nor Secretary Stanton ever publicly declared for national conscription; and no bill on the subject was ever prepared by the administration and presented to Congress. On the surface it appears that the entire project began in the Congress. It is possible that the administration preferred to make national conscription appear to be a result of grass-roots sentiment reflected in the action of the people's elected representatives. However, it seems from the debates that the executive branch may have helped to write the bill, and Lincoln gave it strong support once it was passed. In his message to Congress on December 1, 1862, Lincoln presented the reports of the War Department concerning the military events of the past year and asked Congress to consider them. After Congress had considered the reports, Senator Henry Wilson of Massachusetts, chairman of the Military Affairs and Militia Committee, introduced a bill which outlined the necessity for putting down the rebellion as soon as possible and indicated how it had to be done. Wilson proposed that all persons should be willing to serve in the national army. His bill declared that all male citizens betweeen the ages of eighteen and forty-five constituted the national forces and should be liable for duty when called out by the president.[4]

This National Conscription Bill was a conscious departure from states' rights principles. The national legislature would avoid reliance on the state militia. For the first time the federal government would set up a system under centralized control to satisfy its military manpower needs. It would not rely on volunteers to fill the ranks of the regular army but would draft men. According to Wilson's bill, citizens were a part of the manpower resources of a sovereign state, which made needful rules and regulations for them without regard to state sovereignty. If national conscription were adopted, it would be clear that state sovereignty and theories of federalism had been discarded in favor of national power when it became necessary. Additionally, it would legalize a military policy which would increase pressure toward general abolition and ultimate citizenship status for blacks. Although the Militia Act of July 1862 had removed the racial restriction from federal militia law, there was still no general movement to arm blacks, and some states still excluded them from the militia. If Wilson's bill could be passed and national conscription could be instituted, sentiment for drafting blacks along with other able-bodied males would be intensified. So long as military manpower needs required conscription, the general enlistment of blacks would follow. One newspaper observed that a policy based on necessity might result in general abolition and agitation of the question of black inequality, but for the time being such issues made "not the slightest difference." Even those who were opposed to the use of blacks agreed that conscription had to be tried on "grounds of expediency."[5]

Despite the necessities of the hour, the conscription bill did not become law without a struggle. On February 13, 1863, the Senate resolved itself into a Committee of the Whole and began the discussion. There were thirty-one Republicans, eleven Democrats two Whigs, and two Unionists in the Upper House. Senator Wilson began the debate, basing the legality of the bill on the unqualified power to raise and support armies. This power gave Congress the right to use both voluntary and compulsory processes in defending and protecting the nation. Every nation, said Wilson, has an unconditional right to the service of its citizens for the preservation of the state.[6]

Senator Edgar Cowan, a Republican from Pennsylvania, had no objection to conscription, but felt there were too many exemptions. Cowan maintained, however, that members of Congress ought to be exempt since they were performing duties of more importance to the continuance of the government than soldiers. James Doolittle, a Republican from Wisconsin, agreed with him. Lane, a Republican from Kansas, who had organized a black regiment and who served in the army during congressional recesses, objected. He believed that it was good for the legislators to get out in the field and that they should all set an example by serving during vacations. Cowan's proposal that members of Congress be exempt was rejected.[7]

Senator Cowan then offered an amendment to permit draftees to pay $250 and thus avoid service. He thought that unwilling men would be ineffectual soldiers. Senator Wilson argued that just because a man waited to be drafted it did not necessarily mean that he would be unwilling to fight once he was inducted. Cowan's amendment did not pass, but a later proposal of Senator Daniel Clark, a Republican from New Hampshire, that drafted men be required to hire a substitute or pay three hundred dollars was adopted. This clause of the act, which exempted those who could afford a substitute, made the Conscription Act into a device to aid the well-to-do in avoiding service while seeming to impose an obligation of service on them.[8]

Cowan then proposed that members of state legislatures and governors should be exempted, and this amendment was adopted. Senator Jacob Collamer, a Republican from Vermont, moved that in assigning quotas the number of men already drafted in a particular state should be taken into account, and this proposal was accepted. Senator Wilson added a last section to the bill empowering the president to execute the provisions of the act which was adopted. The bill, passed as amended without a negative vote being recorded, was then sent to the House.[9]

When the Conscription Act was sent to the House, that body was already debating the progress of the war and the need for more manpower. On January 12, Thaddeus Stevens, a Republican from Pennsylvania, introduced a bill calling for the enlistment of 150,000 black volunteers or 150 regiments. This bill was hotly debated for the remainder of January. Representative Samuel Cox, a Democrat from Ohio, made a long, rambling speech in which he traced American military history from the colonial period. He declared that although the regular army statutes permitted their use, blacks had never been enlisted except in emergencies, and no policy encouraging such enlistments had ever been adopted. Although this was an emergency, he thought they should not be used. Cox strongly argued that the Irish would never fight alongside blacks. On February 2, after various representatives offered their conflicting versions of American history regarding the military use of blacks, some declaring blacks had not been used and others that they had, the Stevens bill was passed by a vote of eighty-three to fifty-four. The next day the bill went to the Senate, where Henry Wilson, the chairman of the Military Affairs Committee, was deeply engrossed with his general conscription bill. On February 13, Wilson's committee reported to the House that Stevens's bill would give no new grant of power, since the twelfth and fifteenth sections of the act of July 17, 1862, already empowered the president to use persons of African descent at his discretion in the militia. After all, the War Department was already organizing black regiments in a limited fashion. Wilson apparently felt that the act of July 1862 could be construed to cover whatever additional use of blacks the president thought necessary.[10] Since the regular army statutes already contained no racial restrictions, Stevens's bill would not have expanded the lawful opportunity to use voluntary black enlistees. When Wilson's general conscription bill arrived in the House, it was engulfed in a heated debate, punctuated by invective, on the general conduct of the war. Democratic congressmen, led by Clement Vallandingham of Ohio, insisted on their rights to be heard on the bill. Representative Abram B. Olin of New York, a Republican member of the House Military Affairs Committee, promised that the bill would be debated, but reminded members of the House that a bill must be passed before the end of the session on March 3. If some part of the bill were found to be defective, it could be remedied by a supplemental bill in the next session. The government must, at all costs, have immediate authority to conscript. Olin, without acknowledging the long debate on national conscription during the War of 1812, maintained unchallenged that this was the first time that a national draft had been proposed. Olin argued that it was necessary that the national government exercise its power as a sovereign nation rather than depend on state governors to fill quotas upon the petition of the president. Such dependence was an attribute of a confederacy, not a sovereign central government. Representative Aaron Sargent, a Republican of California, offered the opinion that conscription should have been adopted in 1861. All European nations practiced it, and the Confederacy had been able to raise a huge army from such a small population only by conscripting from the beginning of the war.[11]

Congressman Clinton A. White, a Democrat of Ohio, opposed the bill on the grounds that it would turn the whole nation into a military camp, destroy state sovereignty, and weaken the Bill of Rights, which guarded citizens against summary arrest and arbitrary punishment. Clement Vallandingham argued that the bill was an evil attempt to abrogate the white man's rights in order to alter the status of blacks. If the Union won the war by using blacks, the nation would be nothing more than a military tyranny presided over by a despot. Conscription was necessary only because the public was opposed to the war; otherwise there would be enough volunteers. Daniel Voorhees, a Democrat of Indiana, supported Vallandingham's argument and maintained that people no longer volunteered for the army because the war had become a struggle for the freedom of blacks and the enslavement of white men. If conscription were enacted, a revolution would occur. John Bingham, a Republican of Ohio, opposed both Vallandingham and Voorhees and argued that public opinion supported the war. Further, the measures objected to by the Democrats were necessary if the republic was to protect itself from traitors and revolutionaries.

Congressman Olin attempted to bring the bill to a vote, but his effort was defeated, and the debate continued. Finally, it became evident that

Olin's effort to prevent amendments had failed. Thaddeus Stevens, perhaps the leading proponent of abolition and freedman's rights, proposed to open the bill to amendments for one hour, after which a vote would be taken. His motion was adopted, and Stevens retained the floor to argue in favor of the bill. He believed that national conscription was necessary, in part, because Democrats had successfully conspired to hobble the administration's recruitment drive by assailing the Unionists' aim as a "War for the Nigger." John Steele, a Democrat of New York, thought the bill concentrated too much power in Washington and weakened the state governments. Samuel Cox approved the bill but hoped the first section would be amended in the spirit of the Militia Act of 1792 to permit service only to white men. William Kelley of Pennsylvania thought the first section should be left just as it was, since every man, regardless of color or condition, should be liable to service. John J. Crittenden, a Unionist from Kentucky, felt that the administration had only to abandon its antislavery program, and volunteering would increase to such an extent that conscription would be unnecessary.[12]

The bill was amended to strike out the clause providing for the investigation of "treasonable practices" by provost marshals and add the provision that marshals should detect, seize, and confine enemy spies and turn them over to the commanding officer of the district. The clause concerning draft resisters was amended to require the immediate delivery of such persons to civil authorities rather than their detention by the military until the completion of the draft. Cox's proposal to amend section one to include only white men was defeated by a vote of 85 to 52. The bill was subsequently passed by a vote of 115 to 49. All Republicans except one, Martin F. Conway of Kansas, voted in the affirmative. All Democrats opposed the bill except 2, Edward Haight of New York and Joseph Bailey of Pennsylvania. The border slave state congressmen were evenly divided, 12 in favor and 12 opposed.[13]

When the bill, with the House amendments, was sent back to the Senate on February 28, 1863, the debate continued. Many Democrats took the opportunity to denounce administration policy soundly while barely mentioning the bill in question. Senator James Bayard of Delaware argued that the bill was unconstitutional because it would leave the states without a militia force to protect them against the national government; the bill delegated power to the president which, under the Constitution, only the legislature was to exercise. Senator William Richardson of Indiana predicted that the administration would use the bill to draft heavily from Democratic districts, leaving the Republicans safely at home. Richardson also contended that when an election was held the Democratic soldiers would be confined to camp, while the Republican soldiers would be transported to the polls. Reverdy Johnson of Maryland maintained that if emancipation were sternly disavowed, enough men would volunteer for the service. It would then be "the people's war, the white man's war and a war for the white man's Constitution and his liberty." Senator Willard Saulsbury of Delaware made the final speech on the bill, echoing Johnson's sentiments against the failure to exclude able-bodied free blacks from the national forces. The arguments of Saulsbury and Cox, as well as some of the other Congressmen, expressed the continuing opposition of some border state representatives and peace Democrats to the enlistment of blacks in the military service.[14]

Many Republicans, like Wilson, asserted that the issue was settled by the passage of the Militia Act of July 1862. They insisted that the Militia Act, coupled with the absence of any statute excluding blacks from the regular service, gave persons of African descent the same status as other military eligibles. Military men generally felt that it was necessary to use black manpower, but the Lincoln administration was still hesitating. In any event, the conscription bill was passed with the House amendments on February 28, 1863. The president signed the bill on March 3, 1863, inaugurating the first system of national conscription. Thenceforth, subjection to conscript service, and not a militia obligation, became the badge and moral consequence of citizenship in the nation. Blacks were not excluded from the same obligation imposed upon white citizens. When white men found themselves conscripted, the effort to draft and enlist blacks might take on a new urgency. After all, in a "War for the Nigger," blacks should be the first inducted. The passage of the act gave a new interpretation to the military powers of the national legislature. The power to raise and support armies gave the national government first claim on the services of its citizens. The military clauses of the Constitution did not confine the federal government to dependence on the state to provide manpower for the defense of the nation.[15]

Congressional enactment of the conscription law led to heated public debate, which makes it clear that there was little grass-roots support for the adoption of compulsory national military service, expecially with an exemption for those who could afford to pay three hundred dollars for a substitute. Although it had become evident to administration officials, Congress, and military officials that the manpower had to be enlarged, the public at large was still partly motivated by the belief that conscripts were as bad as convicts. Of course, there were many Democrats who opposed conscription and black enlistments as a part of their program of opposing any measure which might insure Union success. Newspaper columns reflected party biases. Republican and Unionist papers supported the new law, but the Democratic press opposed it.[16] The president made an effort to consolidate sentiment in favor of the measure by issuing a proclamation appealing for public support. Although he never presented it or allowed it to be published, Lincoln prepared a speech in which he lucidly argued for the constitutionality of the draft. Perhaps he simply wanted his opinion to be part of the official record. Lincoln argued that it was necessary to adopt conscription or abandon the effort to save the Union. Decrying the argument that since it acted on individuals and not through the states, the law was unconstitutional, Lincoln pointed to the unconditional grant of power to Congress to raise and support armies. The power was not granted contingently upon the consent of states or the willingness of individuals, but unconditionally.[17]

As soon as the Conscription Act was passed the president initiated a determined effort to recruit as many blacks as possible. If the administration expected the public to accept compulsory service as necessary, all obvious manpower resources had to be utilized. Lincoln ordered the War Department to develop a general policy for the enrollment of blacks. B. Rush Plumly, an officer in the Department of the Gulf, discovered on a trip to Washington in September 1863 that "Mr. Stanton is very urgent about Negro recruiting. The whole thing is the fashion here." On March 15, the secretary of war appointed Robert Dale Owens of Indiana, Colonel James McKay of New York, and Samuel G. Howe of Massachusetts as special commissioners to find ways of inducting blacks. Louisiana, under Union control, was still regarded as the richest recruiting territory. Brigadier General William H. Emory wrote one of his fellow officers in Louisiana that administration officials were "placing too much reliance upon the number and efficiency of the black troops which are raised and to be raised in our Department." The War Department believed such reliance was the best policy. On March 25 Brigadier General Lorenzo Thomas, who was then adjutant general of the United States, was sent on an inspection trip to the Mississippi Valley to examine the condition and use of contrabands and to devise an effective recruiting strategy.[18]

Thomas traveled throughout the Mississippi Valley, visiting Union troops and explaining the desire of the War Department to recruit blacks. His offer of commissions to white privates and sergeants who would command black troops made his mission increasingly more popular. He would name officers and detail them to raise freedmen to furnish themselves a regiment. In May 1863 the Bureau of Colored Troops was set up in the adjutant general's office, and all black troops recruited thereafter were designated United States Colored Troops. The bureau compiled names of persons willing to serve as officers, and Thomas made some of his appointments from their lists. Thomas organized boards to pass on the fitness of candidates for command of black troops and became involved in projects designed to supervise the living conditions of black soldiers, their families, and other fugitives. Commanders like Ulysses Grant, stationed in Tennessee, who had issued orders to turn away fugitives, were now ordered to admit them into their lines. They were even told to prod those who seemed hesitant. Most blacks were still eager to serve, but in some cases blacks were pulled out of their homes or arrested on the streets or plantations and carried off to the army. Henry Johns reported in April 1863, "Many unwilling Negroes are conscripted into the ranks." On August 4, 1863, when a raiding party entered the home of a free Negro to conscript him, he "refused to go and was immediately set upon by the raiders who cut him three times with knives. They then carried him off by force despite the remonstrations of his aged father...." George Hanks reported that such acts occurred "daily." In one effort to end such embarrassing practices, Nathaniel Banks, Commanding General of the Department of the Gulf, ordered all blacks in Union-held parishes enrolled and subjected to the draft. From March to December 1863, they recruited 4,517 black artillerists and 15,488 black infantrymen.[19]

President Lincoln openly expressed a deep commitment to the use of black soldiers. He enthusiastically impressed upon anyone who would listen the necessity for using this "great available and yet unavailed force for restoring the Union." He explained the evolution of his policy in a letter to a "Copperhead" correspondent in Ohio. When Fremont proposed military emancipation in the Department of the West in 1861 Lincoln opposed it because he did not consider it necessary. When Simeon Cameron proposed to General Sherman that he arm the blacks in South Carolina, the president opposed it because it was not indispensable. When David Hunter tried to establish his first South Carolina Regiment of freedmen, Lincoln opposed it for the same reasons. But by March 1862, Union reverses and the absence of a sufficient number of white enlistees made him increasingly aware that the use of black manpower was necessary. That was why he proposed compensated emancipation to the border slave states in March, May, and July of 1862. He wanted to find a way to free the slaves for large-scale military use without pushing the border states into the arms of the Confederacy. The border states rejected his offer; consequently he was forced to act in spite of them. That was why, in 1863, he "laid a strong hand upon the colored element."[20]

After the passage of the Conscription Act, enrollment and drafting were initiated as quickly as possible. If public opinion could be rapidly consolidated behind the movement, Union manpower needs might be met successfully. The military situation dictated all possible speed. Vicksburg had not yet surrendered, Lee was marching into Pennsylvania following the Confederate victory at Chancellorsville, and the Union military future did not seem bright. But the news concerning black soldiers after the passage of the Conscription Act caused increasing optimism. The First and Second Carolina Colored regiments held the Port of Jacksonville, Florida, in April for two weeks "engaged almost everyday with superior numbers of the rebels, and in every instance drove them back." After a severe but victorious engagement against Confederate cavalry and artillery alongside black Union troops, white soldiers in the Sixth Connecticut Volunteers who were "by no means favorable to Negro soldiers" reported that they "had no further prejudices against Negroes who showed such pluck." The Union assault at Port Hudson on May 27 in which the black soldiers of the First and Third Louisiana Native Guards made six or seven charges in the face of heavy Confederate artillery and musket fire, made a "marvelous change in the opinions of many former sneerers." One newspaper observed that the use of black soldiers could be marked down as a success and "their employment . . . may be set down as a military necessity, and no genuine friend of the war can longer object to it."[21]

The news in July of the fall of Vicksburg and Port Hudson, where black troops were heavily engaged in the siege, had a marvelous effect on Northern morale. In the favorable atmosphere created by the Union victories, the draft might be instituted without too much resistance. Conscription was markedly successful in Rhode Island and Connecticut. It was hoped that this feat would be duplicated elsewhere, but such optimism was premature. The Peace Democrats continued to attack the constitutionality of conscription and to point to the unfairness of the $300 commutation clause. Some loyal state governors were discouraged to find the computations of the new provost marshal indicated that they had not satisfied their quotas although their records indicated no deficiencies.[22]

The commencement of the draft in New York City on July 11 resulted in one of the greatest riots in American history. Mob violence dominated the city for three days; arson, robbery, and assault were commonplace. The disturbances were finally quelled on the fourth day by a combination of police, state militia, vigilante groups, and federal troops. Five or six regiments of regular army troops who would have been better utilized in Meade's army, which was in pursuit of Lee after Gettysburg, were called in to aid in suppressing the mob.[23]

The riot was clearly a result of disaffection with conscription, but there were other causes. The open and heated opposition of Governor Horatio Seymour, a Peace Democrat, to Lincoln's policies probably encouraged the dissidents. Southern sympathizers, haters of blacks, criminals, and mischievous youths joined the draft resisters and peaceful demonstrators once the protests began. A major aspect of opposition to the draft which set off the riots was the antipathy felt toward competition from blacks by the laboring classes in many Northern cities. During the riots a crowd raided the draft headquarters, lynched a number of black people in the streets, attacked employers of blacks, and even burned down the black orphan asylum on Fifth Avenue. Blacks had been used as strikebreakers in labor disputes, and during the spring of 1863 there had been several race riots in New York on the waterfront. To large sections of the laboring classes, conscription was a means of forcing white men to fight for blacks, who were their economic rivals. Workingmen did not like being drafted to go South and face Southern bullets to give freedom to blacks while black strikebreakers at home took their jobs. Many workingmen felt that after the war emancipated blacks from the South would infiltrate the North and increase the possiblity of economic competition. If men were to be drafted, in all fairness the despised blacks should be the first to go.[24]

Although the first national draft was strongly opposed almost everywhere, the Lincoln administration vigorously enforced its execution. The brilliant success in New England was not repeated elsewhere. "Copperheads" in other areas seemed determined to follow the example of New York City. Regiments of troops had to be drawn from the forces in the field to enforce the draft in particularly hostile districts. Most military men considered enforcement of the draft worth the effort involved. General William T. Sherman believed that the ultimate peace and security of the country depended on the assertion of the right of that national government to the services of its citizens. General George Meade agreed, declaring that if the administration did not enforce the draft, it might as well make up its mind to a permanent disruption of the Union.[25]

When the first national draft was completed, it was found that of the 292,441 names drawn in the draft lotteries, only 9,881 men had actually been inducted, and that another 26,002 had furnished substitutes. The draft was not important, then, because of the number of men furnished, but rather because of the additional number of volunteers obtained after its institution. Because of the continuing antipathy toward being a conscript, many men volunteered. In some communities citizens raised local bounties and paid men to volunteer to fill their district quota in order to ward off the draft. The law was considered a failure by the provost marshal general because it contained too many escape clauses, exemptions, and ambiguities. Blacks, for example, were in fact conscripted under the law, but the law did not state explicitly that they could be. It was clear that the Congress would soon be asked to provide amendments to the Conscription Act.[26]

The absence of a racial clause in the Conscription Act indicated official understanding of the value of black manpower for a Union victory.

For blacks, however, the implementation of this act meant another major step toward general abolition and citizenship status. Necessity had propelled the Republicans down a road which ended ultimately in the end of slavery. Abolitionist sentiment increasingly bore fruit amid military expediency.

## CHAPTER FIVE

# 1863–JUBILEE YEAR

By the end of 1863 black troops had become a great manpower resource in the Union effort to defeat the Confederacy, and large-scale recruitment efforts were well under way. The Special Colored Troops Division had been organized in the War Department in May 1863 to recruit blacks on a more systematic basis, and after the heroic contributions of black soldiers at Port Hudson, at Fort Wagner and Milliken's Bend in the spring and summer of 1863, more and more black troops were utilized in combat. No longer were they expected to perform guard, picket, and engineer duty but to join white soldiers in engaging the Confederates in the field.[1]

As more and more black soldiers were heavily engaged in fighting, the status of blacks captured by the Confederates became an issue of significant concern. After the Emancipation Proclamation, the Confederate government announced that black soldiers and their officers would be killed, even if they surrendered, or if captured the blacks would be enslaved. Blacks and Northern whites alike demanded prisoner of war protection for black soldiers. A mass meeting of blacks in New York City unanimously adopted and sent to the president a resolution demanding a "policy of retaliation and active guardianship of every enlisted man and every citizen covered by the Federal flag." A *Times* editorial insisted that a Confederate soldier should be killed "for every black loyal private that swings—and that will be but a poor expiation. For a black-skinned loyalist is of more account than a black-hearted traitor anyday." The War Department issued General Order 100, providing that if any black soldier was enslaved, a Confederate prisoner would be executed in retaliation. On July 30, 1863, Lincoln modified the War Department order, so that only when a black soldier was killed in violation of the laws of war would a rebel soldier be executed. For every black soldier who was enslaved or sold into slavery, a rebel soldier would be placed at hard labor on public works until the black was released and treated as a prisoner of war. Union policy was a matter of considerable concern among troops in the field. For example, Lieutenant Oscar Orillion and some of a group of twenty Louisiana Native Guard soldiers on a recruiting mission were captured by a large Confederate cavalry force and hanged and cut to pieces by the rebels. When the report of their fate was received by the regiment, in order to sustain the morale of his men, General George Andrew, commanding Port Hudson, ordered the shooting of ten rebel prisoners in retaliation. The use of blacks as soldiers compelled legal recognition of their equality to whites, at least for the purpose of protecting their status as prisoners of war, in order not to discourage participation in the military effort.[2]

During the last months of 1863 the movement to enlist black soldiers was rapidly gaining popularity everywhere. If enough blacks could be enlisted, fewer whites would have to fight and die. In July 1863 there were thirty black regiments being organized or already in the field. The recruitment of black soldiers had been systematized under War Department control. Camps for the reception and training of black troops had been established at Readville, Massachusetts, Camp William Penn in Pennsylvania, and other places throughout the North. The procurement of officers for black troops was regularized under the control of the Bureau of Colored Troops. After July 1863 the raising of black troops went forward encouragingly. In the Ohio Valley, Union officers made strong efforts to recruit among the free black population. There were regiments being raised in Philadelphia, Washington, D.C., North Carolina, Baltimore, Nashville, Tennessee, and indeed all over the country. The movement had spread from an effort to recruit only Southern blacks to a movement to enlist blacks wherever they could be found. Many Northern states recruited as many resident blacks as possible and sent agents to the South to enlist freedmen who could be assigned to state quotas.[3]

The president was just as anxious to keep the bandwagon rolling as everyone else. He believed that using black troops extensively was absolutely essential for defeating the Confederacy. On July 21, 1863, he ordered Stanton to make renewed and hearty efforts to raise black troops along the Mississippi and elsewhere. On August 9, 1863, Lincoln wrote General Grant that he was sending General Lorenzo Thomas, Commander of the Bureau of Colored Troops, out again and that all commanders were to aid him as vigorously as possible. Lincoln was convinced that if enough blacks were enlisted the Union could "soon close the contest." On August 31, 1863, the president told a correspondent in Ohio that the use of colored troops "constitutes the heaviest blow yet dealt to the rebellion." The president wrote incessantly and talked constantly to anyone he thought might aid the movement. On September 11, 1863, he wrote Andrew Johnson in Tennessee requesting all possible effort on his part to facilitate the raising of black regiments in the state.[4]

State recruiting agents were out everywhere. George Stearns, the abolitionist recruiting agent originally appointed by Governor Andrew of Massachusetts to help recruit the Fifty-Fourth Massachusetts Regiment, was the most successful of their number. Stearns had a widespread organization with subagents scattered throughout the country. On June 13, 1863, he was appointed recruiting commissioner for black troops for the War Department with the rank of major. He raised hundreds of men for the United States Colored Troops within weeks. Soon, however, the operation of the draft, instituted in July under the Conscription Act, interfered with his work. The demand for substitutes for white men who had been drafted attracted large numbers of blacks. The pay for substitution was more lucrative than that for regular army enlistment, which paid no bounty. Stearns was assigned to the Department of the Cumberland and, despite the odds against him succeeded in raising thousands of black troops in Tennessee before he resigned from the service at the end of the year. By the end of 1863 the efforts of the War Department and private recruiting agents had resulted in approximately thirty-eight thousand blacks serving in the Union army.[5]

Although Lincoln had pressed the successful recruitment policy and in the Gettysburg Address clearly stated his goal of freedom as a war aim, the issue of freedom for black soldiers was still unsettled. Blacks were being used to defeat the Confederates; border state people and politicians and Peace Democrats reluctantly acknowledged the fact, but neither they nor most other Northern whites were ready to support the step of abolition and citizenship rights for blacks. Although Frederick Douglass expressed the view of blacks that military service was a first step towards citizenship and freeing of the slaves and the ballot, that thinking was not what a majority in Congress had in mind. At every stage the issue of freedom and citizenship was raised and extensively debated before piecemeal resolution took place. The equal pay question was one such issue.[6]

Black soldiers, successfully recruited and utilized, saw no reason why they were not paid on the same basis as whites. They believed that awarding equal pay would move the national government another step toward enacting freedom and citizenship status for blacks. When, in August of 1862, General Rufus Saxton received War Department authorization to recruit blacks in South Carolina, his orders stated explicitly that black volunteers would receive the same pay and rations as were allowed by law to other volunteers in the service. Volunteers at that time received thirteen dollars per month, including a three-dollar clothing allowance and one ration per day. However, the Militia Act of July 1863 stated that black troops were to receive ten dollars a month including a three-dollar clothing allowance and one ration per day. The authorization given Saxton by Stanton was clearly covered by all statutes regarding volunteers for the regular army passed prior to 1862. There was no racial clause in any of the statutes concerning the regular army, including those outlining pay and clothing allowances. The Militia Act of 1862 was concerned only with persons of African descent who were to be included in labor battalions or in the national militia. The pay provisions of the act of July 1862 applied only to persons raised under that act. However, the War Department paid, or attempted to pay, black troops whether volunteers in the regular army, laborers, or persons serving in the militia units, according to the Act of July 1862. The War Department seemed to think that the act nullified any previous War Department actions or statutes on the subject.[7]

Those persons who attacked the unequal pay accorded to black troops did not do so on the basis of distinguishing between volunteer troops in the regular army and militia units. They argued that the Militia Act of 1862 contemplated the use of blacks mainly in garrisons or on labor battalions. Furthermore, it might have been originally assumed that black regiments would be composed mainly of freedmen and fugitive slaves who performed fatigue duty. But it had become obvious, at Fort Wagner, Port Hudson, and other places that blacks would be used to fight just as white troops did. There was no reason to make a pay differential. It was also obvious that some black soldiers such as the men of the Massachusetts Fifty-Fourth and Fifty-Fifth infantry regiments and the original Louisiana Native Guards were largely free people of color and not former slaves. Also, there were many blacks who might avoid service, even in a "War for the Nigger," if they could expect only unequal treatment, inadequate pay, and no bounty upon enlistment. They might not agree with a newspaper writer that such outrages were a necessary hardship and that to complain of unequal treatment was like refusing "to fight for their freedom until they [were] all elegantly dressed, daintily fed, and applauded as future heroes. . . ."[8]

In May of 1863, as soon as the Bureau of Colored Troops was established, Secretary Stanton asked the Solicitor General of the War Department what black troops should be paid under the law. The solicitor general, William Whiting, apparently studied only the Militia Act of July 1862 without considering statutes concerning the organization of the regular army. He decided that all black troops would be paid ten dollars per month, including a three-dollar clothing allowance and one ration per day.

After his opinion was published in General Order No. 163 on June 4, 1863, General Andrew of Massachusetts insisted that it should not apply to the black men enlisted or mustered into the regular army and went to Washington for talks with Lincoln and members of the Cabinet on the subject. When he was unable to secure immediate action, he asked for and got remedial legislation passed by his own legislature in November 1863, so that the men of the black Fifty-Fourth Massachusetts Regiments could be paid on the same basis as white soldiers, but the black soldiers refused the special appropriation. They believed that all black troops should be paid equal to whites and did not want to be treated differently from other black regiments. It became increasingly evident by the end of 1863 that some action had to be taken to equalize the pay of black troops; otherwise, the recruitment and conscription effort might falter. Secretary Stanton, in his annual report to the Congress, urged the passage of a bill which would unambiguously correct the inequity.[9]

While Congress considered the problem the daily press joined the debate. The *New York Tribune* published a letter written by Colonel Thomas W. Higginson, commander of the First South Carolina Colored Infantry, outlining the injustice involved. Higginson pointed out that not only were black soldiers accorded only ten dollars in pay, but the three dollars for clothing allowance was deducted rather than paid in cash as was the custom with white soldiers. Even Colonel James Montgomery, who had reprimanded the members of the Fifty-Fourth Massachusetts Regiment for not accepting what was offered them, urged the Senate Military Affairs Committee to pass remedial legislation. The *Chicago Tribune* published an editorial outlining the double pay standard wherein a black soldier, no matter what his rank, whether he be chaplain, hospital steward, or sergeant major, received only ten dollars per month, which was less than the pay of the lowliest white private.[10]

When the Thirty-Eighth Congress met in December of 1863 Secretary of War Stanton again recommended that the Conscription Act should be amended to correct the ambiguities involved, including explicit provision for inducting blacks in order to provide for more efficient manpower procurement for the Union army. He also asked that a bill be passed to equalize the pay and emoluments of black soldiers. The draft of 1863, Stanton reported, had been only partially successful. On October 17, 1863, President Lincoln had issued a call for 300,000 additional militiamen to be raised by the states for three years or the duration of the war, but the effort had failed. While many states were still trying to fill their quotas by paying local bounties to blacks and anyone else who would enlist, the provost marshal general asked that a total number of 500,000 men be raised rather than the 300,000 originally called for. Stanton approved of the idea, and on Februrary 1, 1864, President Lincoln issued an order for the conscription of the required men if the states failed to meet their quotas by March 1. Governor Horatio Seymour of New York and other leading Democrats continued to object to conscription. Even loyal Republican governors like Morton of Indiana opposed the continual drain of men from the states which had satisfied prior quotas when states like New York and Pennsylvania remained largely delinquent. Congress had to make some changes in the Conscription Act to equalize the burden.[11]

Democratic Congressmen like Cox of Ohio, Sydenham Ancona of Pennsylvania, and Fernando Wood of New York introduced bills calling for the repeal of the entire act. Their efforts were resoundingly defeated. Senator Henry Wilson of Massachusetts introduced a bill which amended the original act in several particulars, and his bill was finally passed. President Lincoln approved the act amending the conscription law on February 24, 1864. In order to erase any remaining doubt on the subject, an amendment concerning the service of blacks was included in the law. The provision explicitly stated that all able-bodied blacks between the ages of twenty and forty-five years were part of the national forces and liable to the draft. In order to avoid offense to the delicate sensibilities of border state citizens, whenever a slave of a loyal master was drafted, the slave became a freedman and the master was to be paid a bounty of one hundred dollars. Peace Democrats and border slave state representatives criticized the amendment, arguing that blacks were already being drafted and suggesting that Republicans ought to admit that this previous action was illegal. Stevens answered them in the House by asserting that, of course, blacks were already being drafted and it was not illegal. "I do not say it is contrary to law" but rather than leaving an opening for arguments that it was illegal, he preferred "that it be done under a known law." Most of the debate centered on Republican objections to giving compensation to slaveholders under the law. One reason for the explicit inclusion of the clause concerning the service of blacks was the influence of eastern manufacturers, who hoped to buy black recruits. New England textile, arms, and munitions makers were making fortunes from the war and wanted to keep their white workmen in the factories. They wanted no possible hindrance to the substitution of blacks for their drafted men.[12]

While amending the Conscription Act was under discussion, Congress determined to pass separate legislation on the black soldier pay problem. Stanton's report persuaded most members of Congress that the demand for additional troops could only be met by utilizing every available source of manpower. The equalization of pay was, at first, included in a bill to promote enlistments in the service. This measure, introduced by Senator Henry Wilson on January 8, 1864, included a section which guaranteed the same uniform clothing, arms, equipment, pay, and emoluments to persons of African descent as given to other soldiers. Wilson had changed his mind since 1862. His objections had been instrumental in the rejection of an equal pay clause in the Militia Act of July 1862. But now Wilson believed the manpower needs were even more pressing and the pay equalization bill was one way to induce blacks to enlist in large numbers. The bill was brought out of committee on January 18, after the passage of the Conscription Act.[13]

Senator James W. Grimes of Iowa objected to the bill because it included no provision for the payment of a bounty. He suggested that a one hundred dollar bounty be paid, and his amendment was adopted. Further consideration of the bill was interrupted by other matters, and the Military Affairs Committee did not return to the subject for almost two weeks. In the intervening period, Senator Wilson decided that the fastest and easiest mode of adopting pay equalization was by joint resolution. On February 3 he introduced a resolution repeating the language of his initial bill and including the amendment suggested by Senator Grimes. Senator William Fessenden of Maine objected to the retroactive policy envisioned in the resolution. He could see no need to pay troops for services already rendered. Wilson replied that as a matter of simple justice the bill had to be retroactive. Senator John Conness of California agreed with Fessenden and moved to amend the resolution making it applicable only to the period after the passage of the act. Senators James Lane of Kansas and Charles Sumner of Massachusetts immediately jumped to the attack. Lane cited the bravery of his Kansas black troops, and Sumner reminded the senators of the heroic action of the Fifty-Fourth Regiment at Fort Wagner. Senators Fessenden, Grimes, and Jacob Collamer of Vermont continued to object to the retroactive clause. They believed that the government had not explicitly promised to pay all black regiments on the same basis as white troops. In the absence of a general promise there was no necessity for the expenditure of government funds. Senator Wilson decided that compromise might speed passage of the bill. He suggested that the act be amended to make it retroactive only to the first day of January 1864. His amendment was adopted.[14]

Senator James Doolittle of Wisconsin proposed an amendment which would reserve four dollars per month out of the pay of black soldiers to reimburse the government for expenses incurred in feeding and clothing black women and children in the South. This proposal was met with strong objection. Senator James Lane thought that such a discriminatory provision would be an invitation to the rebels to treat black soldiers in a different fashion from white soldiers. If the Union government itself made a distinction, it could hardly complain when the Confederate government decided to treat captured black soldiers as criminals. An effort should be made to abolish all discrimination, not to add other such provisions to the law. Senator Grimes believed it would be unjust to take money from a man to put into a common fund to support persons unrelated to him. Most of the committee agreed with Lane and Grimes. However, before a vote could be taken, Senator Saulsbury of Delaware rose to protest against the constant reference to "colored persons" and "colored soldiers." In Delaware they were called "Negroes" and he wanted them to be so designated by Congress. As soon as Saulsbury could be silenced, a vote was taken on Doolittle's proposal to reserve part of the pay of black soldiers to reimburse the government for the expenses involved in feeding black refugees and fugitives. The proposal was rejected.[15]

Days and weeks went by, and it seemed that the pay equalization bill would never be passed. The passage of the amendments to the Conscription Act, in February, made it even more clear that the majority in Congress thought it necessary to raise as many black soldiers as possible. The war continued doggedly on, and Union manpower losses continued in the thousands. Finally on February 29, 1864, Senator Grimes moved to recommit the resolution to the Military Affairs Committee. Perhaps the Committee could formulate a bill which the Senate would find acceptable.[16]

On March 2 Senator Wilson reported a new bill in the place of the rejected resolution. The first section placed black soldiers on a footing of financial equality with white soldiers from January 1, 1864; the second section offered the same bounty to black troops who were promised it upon enlistment if they were mustered in before January 1, 1864. Senator Garret Davis of Kentucky sought to delay discussion of the proposal by making a long speech on the history of slavery in Europe and the United States and on the Democratic theory that war was still only being waged to save the Union and defend states' rights. When Davis was finally induced to end his oration, he proposed an amendment to the act which would permit compensation for the loyal owners of slaves to be determined by commissioners appointed by the circuit courts. The Conscription Act of February 1864 already provided for the payment of one hundred dollars to loyal masters of slaves who were enlisted in the service. Davis's amendment was rejected.[17]

Congress considered the bill from time to time throughout March, but no progress was made. During the discussions in the House, on several occasions, the question whether the legalization of military service was part of a move toward abolition was debated without resolution. Abolition, according to the Democrats, had led to a drop in volunteering by whites, which led to conscription, which led to the drafting of blacks, which would lead to general abolition. Finally, on April 22 Senator Wilson proposed an amendment to the Army Appropriation Act including his pay equalization measures. He argued that some means of adopting the pay bill had to be found. According to Wilson, not enough black troops were enlisting, and rumors of flagging morale and incipient mutiny and insurrection among black soldiers were reaching his ears. The Senate agreed to incorporate the proposal as a rider to the appropriation bill by a vote of thirty-two to six.[18]

The House of Representatives was still unable to agree upon a bill of its own. On April 30 Thaddeus Stevens asked permission to report the Senate amendments to the Army Appropriation Bill from the Ways and Means Committee. Representative William Holman, Democrat from Indiana, opposed the proposal as another means of imposing a "fanatical and treasonable policy" upon the nation. Holman and other Democrats were unwilling to resolve any issue related to black soldiers without registering their opposition to black recruitment in general. Holman said that it was unwise to use black soldiers in the first place. He claimed they were not being used "to relieve the citizen soldier from oppressive and unaccustomed labor in the hot, sunny fields of the south . . .but you have placed arms in their hands. . . . " He thought that blacks were armed instead of being restricted to labor because that "would not harmonize with your [Republican] political theories." He also asserted that Republicans seemed now to be saying that because blacks were armed they were equal to whites. This had not been stated as the purpose in the beginning. Stevens, in agreeing with Holman's position that the Republicans had not made clear their purpose to arm blacks and make them equal at the time the July 1862 Act was passed, asserted that "we did it very gingerly. We had to wrap it up in such a way that the gentleman from Indiana [Holman] could not use it before his constituents." Kelley of Pennsylvania preferred to focus on Holman's continued objection to the use of black soldiers. He was happy that blacks were being used on the Union side and not on the side of the rebels or out of it altogether. Black soldiers had been "used for the protection of the white man's Government for the protection of the white man's flag, and when so used have fought gloriously in the hope of removing . . . that prejudice which while it has oppressed them has cursed those whom it has controlled."[19]

The House eventually amended the Senate bill in several particulars. The House version set the bounty payable to black troops at one hundred dollars rather than the three hundred dollars authorized under the draft call of October 1863. The Senate amendment authorizing equal payment from date of muster for black volunteers who had been promised it was stricken. A statement assuring all free persons of color the same pay as white soldiers was inserted in its place.[20]

Since the Senate disagreed with the House amendments, a conference committee was necessary. In fact, since the first two were unable to agree, three different conference committees were appointed. On June 10 the third conference committee recommended that the House withdraw its amendment reducing the bounty of volunteers to one hundred dollars; and that all persons who were free on April 19, 1861, be given the same pay, bounty, and clothing allowed to other volunteers at the time of their enlistment. The attorney general of the United States could decide all cases where doubt existed. The secretary of war would be directed to abide by the opinion of the attorney general.[21]

The presentation of the conference committee report initiated further debate. Senator Sumner and Senator Wilson thought it unfair not to provide equal pay for soldiers who were slaves on April 19, 1861. The South Carolina regiments of freedmen organized by Rufus Saxton, even though slaves, had been promised equal pay upon enlistment. There was evidence that they had been awarded equal pay at first but that the War Department had subsequently ordered a reduction. Reverdy Johnson of Maryland and Garret Davis of Kentucky reminded Sumner and Wilson that the Militia Act of July 1862 set the pay of black soldiers at ten dollars per month including a clothing allowance. In any case, they believed that emancipation was payment enough for black soldiers who had been slaves. Senator Fessenden of Maine asked the senators to approve the report since it was apparent that they could agree on nothing better. Senator Wilson agreed that passage of the bill would at least settle the question from January 1, 1864. If the bill was passed as it was now worded, the whole matter would be controlled by the attorney general, and there was no doubt that he would give black troops whatever they claimed. The bill was adopted by both houses of Congress and signed by the president on June 16.[22]

Even while the debate on the pay equalization bill was in progress, Attorney General Edward Bates had prepared an opinion on the black soldier pay problem. President Lincoln had asked him to comment on a complaint of Governor Andrew of Massachusetts regarding the pay of Reverend Samuel Harrison, black chaplain of the Fifty-Fourth Massachusetts Infantry Regiment. Harrison refused to accept the ten dollars offered him and demanded the regular chaplain's pay of one hundred dollars per month.[23] Bates's opinion, issued on April 23, 1864, reviewed the history of the organization of the Fifty-Fourth Regiment and legislative action on the use of black troops. The Fifty-Fourth Regiment had been organized, in the same manner as were other regiments of volunteers, under War Department orders. After reading the statutes concerning the volunteer army and the Constitution, Bates could find "no rule of law, constitutional or statutory" which ever prohibited the acceptance and muster of "persons of African descent" into the regular military service of the United States, as enlisted men or volunteers. One could not, even if still in doubt, construe the statute of July 17, 1862, as limiting the pay of Chaplain Harrison since it referred to the pay of persons enrolled as private soldiers. Mr. Harrison was not a private soldier, but an officer, serving under the commission of the governor of Massachusetts, and mustered into service by the United States government. There was no provision of law, constitutional or statutory, which prohibited the acceptance of blacks in the regular army as private soldiers or commissioned officers. The statutes which declared the qualifications of chaplains did not prohibit the inclusion of persons of African descent. So Harrison was quite legally mustered as chaplain of the regiment. The Militia Act of July 17, 1862, contained a clause which set the pay of chaplains when on duty in the regular or volunteer service at one hundred dollars per month and two rations per day. Although the same act in another section set the pay of persons of African descent employed under the act at ten dollars per month, it was not necessary to find authority for the appointment of Harrison under that act. The Act of July 1862 was clearly intended to cover only those blacks who were enrolled in the militia and called upon to perform fatigue and fortification duty as private soldiers and not to volunteers in the regular army or persons of higher rank and abilities. Bates therefore concluded that Harrison was entitled to full pay and that it was the duty of the president to direct the War Department to pay blacks according to the view of the law outlined in his opinion.[24] The president, however, continued to await the outcome of the debate in Congress.

As soon as the equalization bill became law, President Lincoln asked Bates to provide an interpretation of its provisions. The president wanted to know precisely what bounty and pay were due black troops regardless of their status at the beginning of the war or in January of 1864. Bates prepared a lucid opinion which laid the blame for the doubt and difficulty concerning the pay problem on confusion regarding the Act of July 17, 1862. It seemed clear to Bates that the persons of African descent, who were paid seven dollars per month under that act, were not those persons who were actually mustered into the service for general military duty. That section of the statute referred to the utilization of blacks as laborers. As he had indicated in his opinion in the case of Reverend Samuel Harrison, authority for the pay and enlistment of black soldiers was found in the statute providing for the regular army passed since the institution of the government. By none of these statutes was the enlistment of black soldiers prohibited. Further, by none of the statutes relative to the pay, bounty, and clothing allowance of soldiers was a racial clause included to decrease the amount due to black soldiers. It seemed to Bates, therefore, that any black soldier enlisted before June of 1864 was due the same pay and emoluments as other soldiers. Notwithstanding Bates's opinion, the War Department issued orders to commanders of black troops to indicate what men were free before April 19, 1861, so that they could receive full pay. In most black regiments there were men who were slaves at that time, so the whole problem was solved by administering a "Quaker Oath" to each man. They simply swore that they had owed no man unrequited labor on the day in question and had the notation "free" written next to their names on the muster rolls. This expedient could not be used, however, by regiments composed entirely of freedmen since everyone knew they had been slaves on April 19, 1861. These men continued to be paid ten dollars per month less three dollars deducted for clothing until March of 1865 when remedial, retroactive legislation was passed.[25]

Those whites who, far from the field, expected blacks to be grateful for an opportunity to demonstrate their courage in the hope of obtaining the reward of emancipation from slavery were deluding themselves. Many black soldiers, approximately eighty thousand, were free before the war and had been long engaged in struggles to maintain their status above slavery. The men in the Louisiana Native Guard Regiments who fought so valiantly in the Port Hudson campaign were free people of color before the war. Until after the Port Hudson campaign even the line officers were free men of color from New Orleans, some of whom were wealthy, sophisticated, and well educated. Many were skilled tradesmen and craftsmen, and a few had owned slaves themselves. They had helped to recruit the other Native Guard regiments of freedmen and had promised these men freedom and equal treatment in every respect based upon Benjamin Butler's promises to them. Benjamin Butler wrote a glowing tribute to one of the free Negro officers, Major Francis E. Dumas, one of the largest black slaveholders in Louisiana. Dumas was, Butler asserted:

A man who would be worth a quarter of a million dollars in reasonably good times. He speaks three languages besides his own, reckoning French and English as his own . . . He had more capability as a Major, than I had as a Major General, I am quite sure, if knowledge of affairs, and everything that goes to make a man is any test.[26]

The men of the Fifty-Fourth and Fifty-Fifth Massachusetts regiments likewise consisted mainly of skilled tradesmen and large numbers of the most prominent and respected blacks in communities throughout the North. Only a small number of recruits had been slaves. Frederick Douglass, for example, induced his two sons to join and sounded the call for recruits in his *Monthly*. They were guaranteed by Governor John A. Andrew that they would receive the same pay and emoluments as other volunteers.[27] It was ridiculous to tell men such as these that their reward for fighting and dying in the place of white men who refused to fight was their own personal freedom, or even the freedom of other blacks, and that they who had been fighting discrimination all of their lives should accept discrimination while in the service of the nation. It was only slightly less ridiculous to tell black freedmen, men who had served under the difficult conditions of the war, that the effort was worthwhile to them even while they suffered discrimination and were aware of the ill treatment meted out to their relatives by some of the very Union spokesmen who encouraged them to serve.

These black soldiers had grounds for doubting whether those who promised them freedom could be counted upon to provide it after the war. Occasionally quartermasters refused to issue them supplies and gave them muskets and old uniforms. White soldiers refused to respect black sentries. When brigaded with white troops, black soldiers were frequently forced to perform fatigue duty in addition to fighting while white soldiers rested. As Colonel Henry Frisbie reported in September 1864 of a recruiting trip taken by a group of black and white soldiers near Morganza, Louisiana, blacks were forced to do all of the fatigue duty while "no white troops lifted an axe or spade." The black troops marched as far as they did, did as much guard duty and would probably have fought just as hard." In spite of this, white troops "lay in the shade and watched them work."[28] Despite such treatment many black troops served willingly because they could not risk losing a chance to gain individual self-determination for black people. But they certainly did not regard merely being permitted to fight as reward enough while their relatives suffered in contraband camps, on the plantations, or back home in the North where their men had received no advance federal bounty to cushion the loss of the family breadwinner. An example was Stephen Swails, of the Fifty-Fourth Massachusetts Regiment, who had been a boatman in Elmira, New York, before the war, had been in the forefront of the battle at Fort Wagner, and had received a head wound at Olustee in February 1864 while leading a reconnaissance mission but went on to lead a second successful assault against the enemy. His commander recommended him for a second lieutenancy, which the War Department refused to approve until January 17, 1865, because of his race. Like the other men in the regiment, he received no pay for over a year. Among the stream of letters from families of soldiers complaining about lack of money, he received word in the spring of 1864 that his wife and children were in the poorhouse. When the equal pay bill was passed in July 1864, he accepted thirteen dollars per month, the pay of a private, even though he was performing the duties of a second lieutenant. His family's needs would not permit him to continue to refuse pay as a matter of principle.[29]

The passage of the pay equalization bill indicated national recognition of the continued necessity for using black troops and was another limited step on the way toward civil equality. The day on which the men in the field received their first pay under the new policy was a "day of Thanksgiving and Prayer" as well as jubilation. It was as significant to them as the taking of Atlanta was to the nation.[30] They did not care that many persons regarded the conscription of blacks as a means of simply saving the lives of white men by having blacks killed in their places. They did not care that the major impetus for the passage of the bill was the desire to compensate fairly those engaged in actual warfare and to make military service more attractive to blacks. They believed, like opponents of the bill, that they had yet another basis for claiming recognition as citizens on a plane of equality with white soldiers.

## CHAPTER SIX

# "EARNED" FREEDOM

At every step, legal provisions enacted by Congress to promote the enlistment of black soldiers raised new issues for resolution which made it unlikely that legal slavery would exist for any category of blacks after the war. Promoting the enlistment of black soldiers often required the institution of new policies concerning the even larger numbers of blacks not in the service: the noncombatant men, women, and children. At the beginning of the war, there were some 4 million blacks in the population, and the Union never controlled more than 1 million of these noncombatants at a time. The additional 187,000 blacks in the Union army meant that 2,000,000 remained in areas under Confederate control throughout the war. For the Union each step in mobilizing the black soldiers highlighted the necessity for organizing the fate of the men, women, and children of the civilian black nation. The Emancipation Proclamation, effective January 1863, freeing the slaves in territory in rebellion, also left a potential problem for organizing the fate of those blacks under Confederate control in the event of Union victory. The South, with little dissension, expected blacks to raise food and money crops for the civilian economy and to work for the army as military laborers erecting breastworks, transporting and preparing food and supplies, and to act as body servants. The Confederacy adopted a policy of recruiting blacks for enlistment as soldiers only at the very end of the war. From among the blacks in the areas under Confederate control, some agreed to join the Confederate forces for promises of freedom, homesteads or jobs after the war, not only at the beginning of the war, but near the end of it.[1]

The North acceded to the policy of not interfering with slavery at first and respected the property interest in slaves as reflected in the policy of returning fugitives to their masters. Northerners were Americans too, who had long supported the principle that slaves should never be invited to rebel against their masters. They had joined the South, as Jefferson Davis and other Southerners pointed out, in denouncing "Great Britain in the last and in the present century and in the Declaration of Independence" for violating that principle. But the policy of not involving blacks was short-lived. As soon as the Union army invaded the South, blacks in those areas were either left by their fleeing masters or voted with their feet to join the Union despite army policy. Soon the course of the war required the use of black manpower.

When in May 1861 three male slaves arrived in General Butler's post at Fortress Monroe from the Confederate fortifications where they had been at work, Butler declared them contraband of war and put them to work in his camp. More slaves followed, accompanied by women and children. Everywhere the Union army went came more contrabands "until the stream became a flood." Many thousands of blacks joined this great movement, usually with no possessions except the baggage they carried. The flotsam and jetsam of the Confederacy, including white refugees left behind, added to the endless numbers of those needing aid. In the North, organizations of workers and missionaries mobilized to collect food and materials for their needs. Barracks were erected for temporary shelter, fugitives were encouraged to make contracts for labor on neighboring plantations, and rudimentary hospitals were established for the sick. Gradually fugitives became either organized as a great labor force for the army or remained squatting miserably in refugee camps. From 1862 to 1865 a number of different systems evolved as ways of utilizing the fugitives and promoting the war effort. Some commands provided medicine, rations, and clothing and put blacks to work in kitchens, and as nurses, guides, spies, and washerwomen; some women became paramours of soldiers. The departments of the Surgeon General, Quartermaster, and Commissary utilized some of the men as laborers. Some received allotments and possessory title to abandoned lands. In September 1863 the Treasury Department took over supervision of refugees, fugitives and abandoned lands, and divided the whole Southern region into five special agencies, each with an agent to supervise abandoned lands, labor, and property.[2]

Although blacks within Union lines could be regarded as a supporting resource of the Union army, they could also be regarded as a great nuisance to the war effort. Additionally, most whites, even abolitionists, had prejudiced racial attitudes and considered blacks as an inferior, unintelligent class of human beings. Fugitives deprived the rebels of support and manpower, but the Union had the burden of devising a way to utilize them without jarring the framework of white control while maintaining, insofar as possible, the entrenched patterns of social and economic organization in the South and indeed the entire country. The blacks, consisting mainly of women and children, were especially vulnerable to every manner of trickery, misuse, and degradation. For example, in Virginia, the number of blacks reportedly under federal control rose from about 15,000 late in 1862 to a peak of 70,000 by the end of the war; of these, more than half were female, and no more than 10,000 were enlisted in the army. In order to mobilize the almost 200,000 blacks who actually served in the military, even larger numbers of black noncombatants had to be regulated.

Black labor had to be organized for the task of harvesting the crops of sugar, tobacco, and cotton. A way had to be devised to keep black labor in the field, and the army was the protector and enforcer. Vagrant blacks were expelled from the cities through the use of provost marshal's powers. The object was to obtain laborers for the plantations or soldiers for the army as quickly as they could be absorbed. In many cases Union authorities abused the wives and children of black soldiers in the unhealthy contraband camps or on the plantations in an effort to utilize them as a disciplined labor force. When informed of such abuses some black soldiers tried to "liberate" their families who had been carted off to plantation duty or kept for long periods in filthy contraband camps or arrested as vagrants. Sometimes a group of black soldiers carried out the liberation by marching onto a plantation. This was not always effective, but it was at least as difficult to enforce army discipline under such conditions as it was to prevent Union and Confederate soldiers generally from "skedaddling" or going absent without leave.[3]

The army and the Treasury Department in an uneasy alliance shared the task of organizing black life and labor for most of the war. When Lorenzo Thomas started his recruiting program in the Mississippi Valley in 1863, he described his goal as restoring the prosperity of the plantation economy, protecting the Mississippi River from guerrillas, and returning the freedmen to the land as wage laborers. He wanted every able-bodied male to be a laborer, teamster, or soldier. Those who were unfit for service, along with women and children, would be placed on abandoned plantations. Black regiments would protect the plantations and perform garrison duties, thereby freeing white troops for field service. Black troops, thought Thomas, could operate more effectively than could white soldiers against Confederate guerrillas along the Mississippi. This policy solved the contraband problem and strengthened the North militarily at the same time. In pursuit of this land and labor policy, three commissioners leased abandoned and confiscated lands to persons of "proper" character and qualification. Lessees drew labor from the army contraband camps, posting bond with the commissioners for their employment and good treatment. The lessees agreed to pay males over fifteen $7.00 per month, females of the same age $5.00, and children between twelve and fifteen half the male rates. Children under twelve were not to be used in the field. Hands were often simply denied pay altogether or discovered that they ended up owing the lessee more than they had earned. Thomas responded to criticisms of the policy by asserting that blacks were demoralized because of the disorientations of wartime conditions, and that although the program was hazardous, some disorganization and risk taking in the midst of crisis was to be expected.

Despite federal policy, few blacks became lessees, and federal authorities generally dismissed as fanciful the notion of providing land for blacks. In tidewater Virginia, plantation superintendents rented land directly to a handful of freedmen, and in South Carolina the Direct Tax Commission briefly permitted blacks to preempt plots on estates to be sold at public auction. But in the Mississippi Valley from Natchez to Memphis only about 250 freedmen became farmers in 1864 and 500 in 1865. Only the "best" freedmen—former drivers and others whose training as slaves seemed to qualify them for independent farming—were permitted to become lessees of the Treasury.

The overall conditions of black life in the South during the chaos of war were a mixed reality. The slave narratives describe some of the differing experiences of slaves during the crisis. Some were "running off about this time" not even knowing what the war was about. Some subsisted in the contraband camps. Others stayed with the masters who had treated them fairly before the war. Still others stayed with the master, but when the Yankees came and the "master tried to hide the best stuff on the plantation" the slaves "dat helped him hide it, showed de yankee soldiers, just where it was." Some of the slaves, in isolated areas of states like the "dark corner of South Carolina where the yankees never came," did not know of the progress of the war. For other slaves "run off" to Texas away from the Union forces by their masters, "it was only in 1867, dat us found out us was free; then we all left." Some blacks leased or squatted on government land until they were dispossessed.[4]

About 458,000 slaves remained in the border slave states of Kentucky, Maryland, Missouri, and Delaware. In addition to utilizing slaves in the areas of the South which came under Union control and the approximately 400,000 free people of color in the North for manpower, the Union government decided, based on the February 1864 amendments to the Conscription Act, to draw upon manpower in the border slave states to aid the war effort. In some areas black troops had been raised in 1863 under the Conscription Act or the July 1862 act, which permitted the drafting of slaves of disloyal masters, but applying the taint of disloyalty was a difficult matter. The passage of the act of February 28, 1864, made slaves of loyal masters in the border slave states subject to the draft for the first time. The act explicitly made all able-bodied blacks subject to military service, and loyal masters received a bounty of one hundred dollars for each slave they enlisted. If a slave volunteered for service the master received a three-hundred-dollar bounty. In either case the slave received his freedom. Since blacks could be used to fill up district quotas and the masters could not reasonably object since they were being compensated, many non-slave holding border-state citizens supported the recruitment of slaves. Additionally, before the drafting of slaves in the border states began, many slaves had escaped and enlisted in nearby states, thus aiding those states to fill their quotas.[5] But the large-scale enlistment of slave soldiers in the border states, like other aspects of Union manpower policy, presented the problem of regulating the activities of another large group of blacks, their families and relatives.

Although they received compensation, many slaveholders continued to object to the enlistment of freedmen. They believed the successful use of blacks in the military service brought closer the prospect of general abolition, which they of course opposed. In some places, hostile provost marshals refused to enlist blacks. In counties in Missouri, patrols of slave owners followed companies of blacks going to enlist, intimidating and dissuading them by using violence. In some districts, slaveholders told blacks that if they joined the army they would be placed in the forefront of the battle, their families would starve to death, and that after the war Lincoln would have them reenslaved. Some slaveholders even kidnapped the families of enlistees and sold them into rebel-held territory as an example to discourage other black men from enlisting. A group of slaveholders in Kentucky pursued some blacks on the way to enlist and cut off their ears. Despite efforts to prevent their enlistment, slaves expressed great interest in joining the service. Many marched off the plantations in groups into recruiting stations, others escaped individually in order to join the army. They seemed to have a clear idea that army service was a route to immediate emancipation and citizenship status. They were extremely proud of their uniforms. Some wore miniature flags in their caps to symbolize freedom.[6]

Congress addressed the problems created by the recruitment and freeing of slaves of loyal masters in narrow legalistic terms. Since manpower needs of the army demanded the continued recruitment of freedmen, the issue as they explained it was whether the war effort might be inhibited because of threats against the families of black soldiers who remained in bondage. Some provision, clearly, emancipating these relatives seemed to be necessary. In January of 1864, Congress originally considered the problem when Senator Henry Wilson introduced a bill to promote enlistments and equalize the pay of black soldiers. The third section of that bill declared that when any slave was enlisted into the army or navy, he, his mother, wife, and children were forever free. When the bill was considered by the Senate, border slave state senators strongly opposed it. Senator Lazarus Powell of Kentucky moved to strike out that section.[7]

Powell's motion initiated a long debate. The Democrats generally framed the issue, as all others related to slavery and the war, in terms of protection of property and states' rights, and the Republicans argued in terms of military necessity and humanitarianism. When Senator John Henderson of Missouri proposed that the family of the slave should be declared free only if his owners aided the rebellion, Senator Grimes of Iowa reminded Henderson that he was only repeating the law on the subject in the Conscription Act of 1862. Grimes supported the emancipation of relatives of soldiers because he believed that the military service of such persons was a fair exchange for the property involved. Senator John Carlile of Virginia asserted that their owners could legally emancipate slaves. If slaveholders in the Confederacy and the border states found it necessary to do so, they could arm and emancipate slaves. According to Carlile, the war had not transferred the disposition of slave property from control of the states to the national government.[8]

The debate continued throughout the months of February and March without reaching a conclusion. On March 18, 1864, Senator Wilson moved to strike out the entire section of the bill and insert a clause providing for the compensated emancipation of the relatives of slave soldiers. Senator John Sherman of Ohio proposed that the whole subject be postponed so that attention could be given to the Thirteenth Amendment proposal abolishing slavery. If slavery were speedily abolished throughout the country, this bill to emancipate legally the families of soldiers would be unnecessary. Senator Sumner objected on the grounds that the need for the bill was immediate, while the amendment might not be adopted for months. Senator Grimes and Senator B. Gratz Brown of Missouri, correctly, agreed with Sumner. Lyman Trumbull had introduced his abolition amendment into the Senate in March, and it was passed thirty-eight to six on April 8, 1864, but was tabled in the House by a vote of ninety-five to sixty-five in June. Then, Senator Sherman reminded the Senate that since black marriages were not legalized, it might be extremely difficult to determine who the relatives of slave soldiers were. He recognized that one of the harsh realities of slavery was that, despite ties of love and affection, blacks had little opportunity to preserve family unity and stability. Senator Grimes and Senator Jacob M. Howard of Michigan suggested that for purposes of the emancipation proposal they might simply ask the soldiers to identify their acknowledged spouses and children.[9]

Throughout April and May the Senate considered the bill but was unable to come to any agreement. Senator Waitman T. Willey of West Virginia suggested that the violence and intimidation suffered by the families of slave soldiers in the border states was not a result of objection to slave enlistments. He felt that such actions could be attributed to the exasperation of the masters with the prospect of general abolition. If the subject were left alone, perhaps the violence would cease. Despite the attempts of its proponents, who tried every means to effect agreement, the bill failed to pass before the end of the session.[10]

In the summer of 1864, the war still seemed far from a conclusion. Many Northerners began openly expressing a desire for peace at any price. An attempt to conclude the war on terms that might include reenslaving freed blacks might incite race warfare, but there was a possibility that emancipation could be reversed by a court decision that Lincoln's proclamation was illegal, by a negotiated peace, or a Republican loss in the 1864 elections. Lincoln even discussed with Frederick Douglass, on August 10, the possibility of finding a way to urge blacks to escape prior to any negotiated peace. By the time Douglass responded three weeks later that such a project of escape was unfeasible, General Sherman had won Atlanta, Admiral Farragut had captured Mobile, and a negotiated peace no longer appeared possible. In November, Republican Unionists swept the elections easily.

On December 13, 1864, the supporters of the measure to free the families of slave soldiers took up the subject again. Senator Wilson introduced a joint resolution embodying the substance of his original proposal. Since the passage of the act to amend the Conscription Act in February 1864, thousands of additional freedmen had been enlisted. Almost a year later, the Union government had made no legal provision for the emancipation of the families of slave soldiers. Moreover, Wilson explained that from seventy-five to one hundred thousand wives and children of black soldiers whose services the government could not dispense with without imperiling the nation were still in slavery. The Democratic Senators were still adamant. Senator Hendricks of Indiana sought delay by proposing that the resolution should be referred to the Judiciary Committee. He felt that Congress would be violating the Constitution if it freed a servant held to service by the laws of a state. Senators Lazarus Powell and Garret Davis of Kentucky agreed with him. Davis asserted that the proposal was not only unconstitutional but inhumane. It would deprive slave families of the support of their masters and reduce them to beggary for their support. Senator Samuel Pomeroy of Kansas, in arguing against Davis's objection, said that he had seen emancipated slaves in Missouri and the District of Columbia. They did not seem to be starving or to be in a worse condition than many poor white persons. Senator Wilson reminded the Senators that black soldiers received pay of sixteen dollars per month. He saw no reason to suppose that they would refuse to support their wives and children.[11]

When the joint resolution was passed by the Senate by a vote of twenty-seven to ten and referred to the House of Representatives, many Democrats hoped it would die in the Judiciary Committee, but it was reported without amendment on February 22. The border slave state congressmen immediately attacked the constitutionality of the measure. Representative James F. Wilson of Iowa staunchly defended it from all attackers. Wilson expressed the view that the Congress could pass whatever legislation it deemed necessary and proper to prosecute the war. This act was necessary to gain manpower for the army and to relieve the minds of black soldiers from worry over the fate of their relatives. It was a humanitarian act within the legal authority of Congress under the war powers, and there was no need to await the adoption of the Thirteenth Amendment to reward soldiers by freeing their relatives. Indeed they should be freed as a boon to the soldiers even if the Thirteenth Amendment were not ratified. The resolution narrowly passed the House by a vote of seventy-four to sixty-three and was signed by President Lincoln on March 3, 1865. The passage of the Thirteenth Amendment crippled the opposition against its enactment, but the state courts of Kentucky continued to ignore the federal statute and recognized the existence of bondage for the relatives of black soldiers until the Thirteenth Amendment was ratified. Those congressmen who believed that black soldiers did not recognize family ties need not have worried. Evidence that family recognition was a strong motivating factor among the slaves became immediately apparent. Once freed, slaves maintained legally the two-parent family structure of their former masters, and the black family continued to be a patriarchal institution about as stable as the white family.[12]

Once freedom for the families of slave soldiers was enacted into law, it appeared that Union governmental policy to provide black manpower for the war effort had been completely elaborated. However, the pay question remained still not completely resolved. Even after the passage of congressional acts equalizing the pay of black troops, administrative officials did not easily adjust to implementing the new policy. When the war ended many black troops discovered at muster-out, after a period of long and honorable service, that army officials attempted to discharge them without paying a just bounty. In July 1864, Attorney General Bates issued an opinion explaining that pay and bounty equal to that given white soldiers should be paid to black troops, and he directed the War Department to abide by his opinion. In March 1865, after the Thirteenth Amendment had been passed, Congress hastily enacted a statute equalizing the pay of slave soldiers so that there would be no problem at muster-out. But, when the time actually came to dispense the bounty due from enlistment, some War Department officials procrastinated.

On September 20, 1865, the Secretary of the Treasury, Hugh McCulloch, wrote to Attorney General James Speed, asking for another opinion on the subject. McCulloch wanted to know whether appropriating money from the treasury to pay the bounty of one hundred dollars to former slave soldiers was lawful disbursement. Speed referred McCulloch to Bates's opinion as a controlling statement on the subject. Speed thought perhaps Bates's opinion could not be stretched to cover even those men who were slaves on April 19, 1861, so he offered his own interpretation of their rights to payment. He explained that any slave of a rebel master who became free as a result of section 10 of the Confiscation Act of July 17, 1862, became automatically subject only to the statutes which concerned free men. The fact that he had once been a slave was not relevant. This class of former slaves became soldiers under the statutes relating to the regular army, which made no mention of color or servitude, and should be paid the amount as white soldiers were.

Another class of soldiers who had been slaves were those freed under the provision of the Emancipation Proclamation. According to Speed, at the instant they became free they qualified to become volunteer soldiers, competent to enter into valid contracts of enlistment in the National Army. Their contracts should have been based on the same provisions applied to white soldiers. Since no law prior to the Act of June 15, 1864, stated special rates of compensation for the service of blacks, any black person, whatever his previous condition, who enlisted in the service before June 15, 1864, was due the same pay and bounty as other troops.

Since the Act of June 15, 1864, entitled only those blacks who were free at the time of their enlistment to equal pay, one might infer that slave soldiers were not included in the act's provisions. Speed maintained that the Congress could not have intended to violate both the legal and moral obligation of the contracts entered into with these men under all previous statutes applying to service in the regular army. The bounty clause of the act of June 1864 provided that black soldiers mustered after the passage of the act would receive whatever bounty the president ordered not exceeding one hundred dollars. That provision was, however, repealed on July 4, 1864, by a statute which provided for the payment of a graduated bounty to all volunteers based upon the terms of their respective enlistments. Speed concluded that all black soldiers freed under the Confiscation Act of July 1862 and mustered in before June 15, 1864, should be paid whatever bounty white volunteers enlisted during the same period received. Fugitive slaves of rebels emancipated after July 17, 1862, and enlisted before June 15, 1864, were also entitled to the bounty payable by law to volunteers. Black soldiers mustered after June 16, 1864, were entitled to a sum set by the president not exceeding one hundred dollars, and all black volunteers enlisted after July 4, 1864, should receive the same pay and allowances as white soldiers enlisted at the same time.[13]

Despite the passage of the Enrollment Act of July 4, 1864, and contrary to Speed's opinion, most black troops received only a one-hundred-dollar bounty at muster-out without regard to enlistment dates. The paymaster told them this was all they were owed by the government. In most cases free blacks recruited in the North were granted state bounties of fifty dollars and more, which somewhat cushioned the shock of receiving no federal bounty for enlistment upon discharge. The regiments of freedmen recruited in the South received no state bounty, of course, and in fact received little for their service in the war. If their freedom could be maintained, this might be regarded by the black soldiers as adequate payment for their services. On June 15, 1866, Congress passed a statute which explicitly stated that the omission of the words "free on or before April 1861" did not preclude the payment of a bounty to any soldier. In the same statute, Congress provided for the payment of pensions to families of deceased black soldiers, even in the absence of a legal marriage. For pay purposes, the wives and children of such persons were those persons to whom they had shown some obligation. In most cases, evidence that the soldier had sent money home to a particular person was sufficient.[14]

When the Civil War ended there were almost 200,000 black troops in the Union army out of a total Union strength of 797,807 men, and of the Union war dead, approximately 38,000 were black troops—a mortality rate 35 percent greater than among whites although blacks entered the war in large numbers much later. Black regiments fought in 449 encounters with the Confederates, 39 of which were designated as major battles. Seventeen black soldiers and 4 black sailors received the Congressional Medal of Honor. Black manpower had tipped the balance toward victory for the Union army. The statute books contained provisions for the continued service of blacks. The president and the Congress had encouraged and sanctioned black enlistments. The statutes concerning the service of blacks had been interpreted favorably by the attorney general of the United States and the judge advocate general of the War Department. Even the Confederacy had resolved finally to enlist blacks. In future American wars, there would be no doubt that blacks could be lawfully enlisted. The problem in the Civil War was one of legalizing a policy that was dictated by the need for troops to defeat the Confederacy. In the next wars it would be a question of propriety and necessity rooted in a remembered legality.

## CHAPTER SEVEN

# FREEDOM FOR THE FREEDMEN

When Lyman Trumbull, Republican from Illinois, introduced in the Senate his amendment abolishing slavery in March 1864, the Union still required the use of large numbers of black soldiers in combat in order to defeat the Confederacy. Trumbull's bill was passed in the Senate by a vote of thirty-eight to six on April 8, 1864, but tabled in the House, by a vote of ninety-five to sixty-five, in mid-June. In January 1865, when the bill came up for reconsideration, black regiments were involved daily in efforts to end the war, then in its final campaigns. The Democratic opposition again, as in the previous June, held the power to deny the abolition amendment two-thirds approval. Partly through the efforts of William Seward and his lobby of moderate Democrats, a few Democrats did not vote and sixteen Democrats voted for it, and the amendment was passed. A Republican two-thirds majority in the next Congress guaranteed its eventual passage. In addition to possible use of money and patronage, the Seward lobby promised recalcitrant Democrats generous peace terms to the South, speedy full reinstatement of the South in the Union and continued cooperation between conservative Republicans and moderate Democrats. The administration argued that passsage of the amendment would hasten peace and insure its permanency. Democrats and moderate Republicans saw the amendment as settling the slavery question and permitting the formation of new conservative political alliances of Republicans and Democrats on other issues. By early 1866 most Republicans and the public were committed to the idea that a Civil Rights Bill was necessary in order that the Thirteenth Amendment would not be a sham. Equal rights without suffrage was their position. Johnson and Seward, in the interest of creating a new party and isolating the radicals, opposed what turned out to be a majority.[1]

In fact, the Republicans were solidly together on the race issue. Some Republicans wanted equal suffrage for blacks; men like Ohio's John A. Bingham, Charles Sumner of Massachusetts, Thaddeus Stevens of Pennsylvania, and Jacob Howard of Michigan, but they submerged their concerns to mesh with the party position in 1865 and 1866 of equal rights up to suffrage. Also the issue of the basis of representation in Congress after abolition, even without black suffrage, occupied the Joint Committee of Fifteen on Reconstruction all during early 1866. Republicans were concerned about maintaining control of politics, about public hostility to increasing the power of the South, about providing legal protection for Republicans in the South, and about national safety as well as what measures would enable blacks to protect themselves from reenslavement. But first came the adoption of the Thirteenth Amendment and the Civil Rights Act of 1866 as the first enacted legal means for insuring black protection. In addition to such factors as humanitarian interest in black freedom and anger toward the South, which in seceding had caused the shedding of blood to maintain the Union, one of the important political reasons for the adoption of the Thirteenth Amendment and the Civil Rights Act of 1866 was Republican military policy during the war. The work of the Seward lobby more easily bore fruit because the tug of military expediency, which required the emancipation and the recruitment of black soldiers, moved the national government ever closer to a requirement that legal rights, including suffrage, had to be provided for blacks.[2]

Republicans, in early 1865, expressed continued awareness of the connection between military policy and the black equality problem in debates on abolition issues. In the Senate in January, Republican James R. Doolittle of Wisconsin, opposing a bill to free the families of slave soldiers in the border slave states, objected that the bill was unnecessary because adoption of the Thirteenth Amendment would free all slaves. Since by that time even Jefferson Davis in the Confederacy proposed limited abolition as a war measure, Senator Doolittle did not see how the House could fail again to adopt abolition as they had the previous June. Henry Wilson, Republican of Massachusetts, responded that the blacks against whom "outrages" were being committed could not wait for the passage of the Thirteenth Amendment. But still with an eye on military needs and the war powers as a constitutional basis for legislation, he said the bill was necessary because "we owe it to the course of the country, to liberty, to justice, and to patriotism to offer every inducement to every black man who can fight the battle for the country to join our armies." Willard Saulsbury, still embittered by the continued failure of the states' rightist argument against military use of blacks, argued that the modern doctrine of "military necessity" could not be extended to mean that in a state of war "whatever the Congress of the United States shall decree, is constitutionally decreed." Sumner responded that slaves had been used and freed and now "intrinsic justice and humanity" dictated freedom for the families of slave soldiers.[3]

In early 1865, when the House discussed the president's annual message including strong support of abolition, John A. J. Creswell, Republican from Maryland, squarely faced up to the race question. He said that "the stern necessity of self-defense" lent support to the Emancipation Proclamation. After two years time, the people made it clear in the November 1864 elections that they desired to "dispel all legal doubts, and make that proclamation good for all time, and universal in its application by amendment of the Constitution." If there was a governmental obligation to protect slavery before the war, "that obligation has been forfeited." He had heard that even the Confederacy wanted to use black soldiers. If so, they would learn like the Union that "men who have handled muskets do not willingly become slaves." Blacks would have to remain free or be forcibly returned to bondage. Glenn W. Scofield, a Pennsylvania Republican, in supporting him, stated that he did not see why slavery should "linger in party warfare through a quarter or half of a century of monotonous debate, patchwork legislation, and conflicting adjudication." They should be done with it, in conformity to the will of the people.[4]

When the abolition amendment itself was debated in the House on January 9, 1865, George H. Yeaman, Union party representative from Kentucky, expressed the view that the Democrats should get on the right side politically in order to exercise power in the future by "cutting loose from a dead carcass." He thought that everyone would recognize that compensation, giving lands to blacks or giving them citizenship, was not really the issue. If anyone suggested continuing the war one hour "for such fruitful and malignant ends" they would be silenced. He believed that "schemes" directed toward compensation, giving land or citizenship and suffrage to blacks and the like would be universally "abandoned" once the abolition amendment was passed. Furthermore, he thought that slavery was at an end no matter what they did and even if the South won the war. There would be, under arms, former slaves "who have been *contracted* with, been armed and drilled, and have seen the force of combination." Not only would they not be returned to slavery, they would "leaven the whole mass" of slaves who had not been in the military; "their mere presence, the idea, if their mouths were padlocked would soon have this effect."[5] Yeaman's efforts in support of the amendment, stimulated in part by the direct influence of Lincoln, was apparently rewarded. He was appointed minister to Denmark in 1865. Robert Mallory, a Kentucky Democrat who opposed Yeaman, argued that the abolition amendment would create the further difficulty of deciding what to do with the blacks. Mallory predicted that the Republicans would use blacks as voters in the South for the purpose of keeping control of the national government and the Southern states. He got little support for his argument in the debate that day.[6]

On January 11 and 12, as the debate continued in the House, the Democrats focused on constitutional arguments. Democrat William S. Holman of Indiana sought to frighten supporters of the amendment by raising the spectre of suffrage. He explained that abolition was the "entering wedge" for a bill that gave civil rights to blacks on the theory that they would not be secure unless they were citizens who could vote. Indiana Democrat James A. Cravens suggested that since Northerners were opposed to an influx of black immigrants into their states, and colonization was apparently not in the cards, abolition would mean domination by black majorities over whites in the South. Massachusetts Republican George S. Boutwell and Ohio Democrat George H. Pendleton, asserting that the amendment was unconstitutional insisted that slavery had been an initial condition of ratification to the Constitution. The Constitution would itself become illegal if a basic unamendable particular of it concerning slavery was discarded. Illinois Republican John F. Farnsworth reminded Pendleton that he had voted in 1861 to add an amendment which prohibited abolishing slavery. If it was possible to amend the Constitution on the slavery question in 1861 it should be possible to amend it in 1865. Pendleton responded weakly that an amendment to keep slavery forever was legal, but not an amendment to get rid of it.[7]

On January 12, 1865, after Green Clay Smith, Union representative from Kentucky, explained that he would vote for the amendment because after the war the black soldiers could be marched into Mexico to drive out Napoleon III, Samuel S. Cox, Ohio Democrat, electrified the House by supporting the Republicans on the issue of constitutionality. Cox, who had been approached by the Seward lobby and was wavering, although he finally voted against the amendment, entered the continuing dispute between Pendleton and James M. Ashley, Ohio Republican, over whether slavery was a nonamendable preexisting condition of the Constitution. According to Cox, his fellow Democrats were just using the Constitutional arguments in order to support their objectives. He thought that it was of course constitutional to amend the Constitution but that a supportable reason for Democratic opposition was that abolition was "inexpedient" and "anarchical."[8]

On January 31, after the final plea against the amendment by William H. Miller, Democrat of Pennsylvania, who thought they "should not pull down the old house until we have built the new one," the House passed the amendment. The vote was 119 to 56, with eight Democrats absent. The bill was returned to the Senate and sent on to the president, who signed it on February 1, 1865. Afterward on February 4, 1865, Trumbull and the Senate went on record that since a constitutional amendment did not need a presidential signature before being sent to the states for ratification, the bill had been mistakenly forwarded to the president. When the amendment passed, during the last tough months of fighting, there were some 200,000 blacks in the army, including the all-black Twenty-Fifth Army Corps of thirty-two black regiments that had been organized in the Army of the Potomac in December 1864. In the last year of the war black troops made up large contingents in almost every successful battle in the Department of the South. The Thirteenth Amendment had been passed by the Congress but the legal issue of freedom and equality for soldiers and the masses on whom they would act as "leaven" was not yet resolved.[9]

Aside from the reports of General Ulysses Grant, Carl Schurz, and others on conditions in the South, politicians received information from constituents who were still in the military services on the behavior of Southerners toward the freedmen. For example, a soldier in Hilton Head, South Carolina, told Lyman Trumbull in May 1865 that the Southerners were planning to "put the colored man who has been so true to us, way out of reach of Justice." The only remedy was a continued military presence, including black soldiers. Another soldier in Meridian, Mississippi, suggested that although the North was opposed to it, more than black suffrage was needed. Blacks would not be permitted to vote anyway, "whatever may be the laws on the subject," if the military garrisons were removed. True, the black masses did not really have the wherewithal or knowledge to fight against oppression like revolutionaries in England or Europe, but "with good leaders, they will fight to the death."[10]

By the time the next Congress met in December 1865 and Andrew Johnson had sent his annual message to Congress, events had moved quickly to make resolution of the issue of legal rights for blacks even more crucial. Lincoln had been shot, and the war was ended. A period of confusion and uncertainty about Reconstruction and the programs of the new president ensued. Democrats sought to gain Johnson's support for a new conservative coalition to oppose the Republicans. Like Lincoln, Johnson made ratification of the Thirteenth Amendment a condition of readmission in the South. But, South Carolina, Alabama, and Florida, in ratifying the Thirteenth Amendment, provided that the second section did not give Congress the power needed after the Civil War to determine the political status of slaves. This position was expected, since Seward had in November written just such an interpretation to the provisional governor of South Carolina. Johnson and the administration seemed to agree with white

Southerners that the Thirteenth Amendment was an end and not a beginning. Many Republicans, although not committed to suffrage, supported civil equality and opposed increasing the political power of the South while blacks were held close to slavery. Blacks themselves wanted nothing less.[11]

What to do with the blacks was still an unresolved issue. If Northern states' responses served as a guide, few gave blacks the suffrage. Congress tried to develop a procedure for protecting the rights of blacks without unnecessary interference with states' rights. The second section of the Thirteenth Amendment, which gave Congress the power to enact appropriate enforcement offered the opportunity for this development. The Civil Rights Act of 1866, based on the second section of the amendment, left the way open for the states to enforce civil equality without the injection of a federal presence unless necessary. The act prohibited both state and private interference with civil rights. Along with the Freedmen's Bureau Bill extension, protecting army officers and blacks in contracts and in certain judicial contracts, the Civil Rights Act was a limited effort to obtain enforcement of black rights. The two bills emitted from a majority concern that freedom for blacks not be a sham but that there not be too much intrusion into state power.[12]

Still, throughout 1865 and into 1866 as Congress discussed the format of acceptable civil rights legislation, black soldiers remained an ominous presence. In July 1865 there were 123,156 black troops in the army, 120 regiments of infantry, and 12 regiments of cavalry. White men were being rapidly mustered out; they were anxious to go home, and any delay was questioned. Black troops were more willing to stay in the service because their terms had not expired, and most of them did not have a home or employment to return to. Those opposed to the presence of black troops in the South, especially when they outnumbered whites, argued that blacks had not been in service as long and were less well-trained and disciplined. Some whites cited cases of mutiny (resulting in many instances from black soldiers' perceptions of racist treatment on the part of white officers) as a basis for declaring black troops unsuitable. White citizens complained about the uppity behavior of armed blacks. Commanders tried when possible to isolate black troops by stationing them in remote garrisons.[13]

Generals protested each time they received muster-out orders from Washington if more black than white regiments remained in their areas. Generals Ord and Halleck, offering incompetency and discipline as reasons, removed the all-black Twenty-Fifth Army Corps from occupation duty in Virginia. They reported complaints that black soldiers were hostile to whites, sometimes insulting them, that they allegedly raped some white women, and that they encouraged militancy and insolence among the civilian blacks, who were expected to remain docile. A good example of the kind of complaint the whites thought justifiable is this telling report of General Gillmore:

I have found so many bad men among the noncommissioned officers and privates of some of my colored regiments—men who by their false representation and seditious advice, have exercised most baleful influences upon the plantation laborers—that I have been forced to devolve upon the white troops—to a much greater degree than their numbers would justify—the obvious and delicate duties of instructing the inhabitants of the country in their rights and responsibilities as well as the ratifying and enforcing of labor contracts. In many instances nearly all the laborers on large plantations under extensive cultivation have violated their contracts and suspended their work in consequence of the permissive influence of a few bad colored soldiers, who were formally slaves in the community.

After experiencing slavery, warfare, unequal pay and work assignments, conceivably black soldiers were militant and indeed acted as a yeast in developing consciousness among the civilian black population. Gillmore did not encourage the discharge of black soldiers from the service, because he feared they would be free to create even more militancy and discontent among black freedmen in the local community.[14]

In September 1865 Grant successfully urged Stanton to order the muster-out of all black regiments raised in the North. Grant assumed that those raised in the North in volunteer regiments were a greater source of difficulty, since they were unfamiliar with Southern racial ways. During the last half of 1865, when President Johnson made the Thirteeth Amendment a condition of readmission to the Union, and the first months of 1866, when Congress enacted the Civil Rights Act and Freedmen's Bureau Bill, the proportion of black to white troops in some parts of the South was three to one or higher. The order to muster out numerous white volunteer regiments in August 1865 left General Stoneman in Tennessee two batteries of white artillery and thirteen black regiments of all arms. Five of these black regiments were ordered to Alabama, where at that moment white troops were in the majority, so that General Woods could muster out five white regiments. In December 1865, when the states formally ratified the Thirteenth Amendment, only one of twelve infantry regiments in Mississippi was white, and in the following month there were 6,550 white and 17,768 black volunteers in Texas and Louisiana. Not until November of 1866 was black military strength after muster-out at a low enough level to make black military presence in the South a non-threatening issue, and even then the presence of black veterans remained threatening.[15]

Black troops in the field experienced daily their influence on the attitudes of white and black populations, and even some white Northerners became concerned about the possibility of an explosion. One Ohio resident told Secretary of War Stanton in January that abolition was inevitable: "It would require a power vastly greater now to arrest them [blacks] than it will to consummate the movement," but he feared for whites in the South that "armed Africans" among the depleted population of the South would "be masters of the situation," and that "scenes of San Domingo may be reenacted." When the Fifty-Fourth Massachusetts Regiment marched through South Carolina in the Georgetown area on April 20, 1865, about three thousand black civilians eagerly followed them. When the soldiers arrived at Charleston, where they were assigned to guard and picket duty for the next four months, large numbers of blacks surrounded them wherever they went. The commanders of the Louisiana Native Guards, assigned to guarding railroad stations at Terre Bonne in the last year of the war, ordered them not to peer into the windows of the trains or to speak to the white passengers, who felt threatened by their presence.[16]

The army and white Northerners and Southerners alike regarded black soldiers as a threat to white Southerners. At no time during the period when Congress debated endlessly the issue of abolition did information from the field indicate any feeling that slavery could be imposed, without bloodshed, on the black men in the army, or on the surrounding black population. Democrats in Congress might argue unconstitutionality, inexpediency, futility, and danger in opposition to abolition, and the Republicans might seriously respond; but these debates were not echoed from soldiers and commanders in the field. The end of slavery was irrevocable. Some settlement that would maintain the peace, which would make blacks believe their rights were being acknowledged and whites resign themselves to civil equality, was necessary. The muster-out and disarming of black troops required breathing space. In Louisiana, General Canby, deviating from long-standing army procedure, at Grant's directive, ordered that black soldiers, being discharged from the army, should not be permitted to purchase their weapons to take home. The generals hoped to disperse the influence of black soldiers more widely in order to dissipate the effect of their militancy, and to arrange for the transfer of the remainder to the West, where they could be occupied with fighting the Indians and defending the frontier.[17]

Black spokesmen and soldiers made clear from the beginning that they expected military participation in the war to hasten abolition and equality for black people. Since the war came and the South unabashedly fought to maintain slavery, they supported the Union effort in the hope that the course of events would lead to abolition. In any case, given the South's defense of slavery, they had to support the Union. Depending on their circumstances blacks focused on abolition, improved economic conditions, education or civil rights—including the right to vote—as objectives in the war. Slaves and freedmen expected the war to bring individual freedom, economic conditions of life, food, clothing, and shelter that were at least as good as they had been provided by the master before the war, as well as the opportunity to own land, acquire an education, and exercise political freedom in that order. They had no reason to believe that Northern whites intended to leave them economically more deprived than they had been as slaves. They placed importance on the other items because the culture in which they lived as slaves had placed principal emphasis on their possession. They believed the Union would grant either the provision of land and education or the wherewithal to purchase them. Of course, Southern planters hoped to depart as little as possible from antebellum conditions after the war. Northern businessmen, philanthropists, and politicians, as concerned about preserving property interests as the Southerners, generally opposed confiscation of Southern plantations and the carving of homesteads out of them for the freedmen. The position of most whites North and South meant that the experiments in alloting abandoned properties to freedmen during the war generally did not survive the claims of the former rebel owners, and that sharecropping and crop lien systems evolved. Instead of receiving reparations payments or forty acres and a mule outright, freedmen often found themselves as deprived economically in terms of food, clothing,and shelter as they had been before the war.

The experiments in allocating land in the Sea Islands of South Carolina in 1862 and again by Sherman's Order No. 15 in 1865 ended when after the war Johnson restored most of the land to former owners. Similarly in Mississippi at Davis Bend on Jefferson Davis's plantation, the land leased to blacks reverted to 140 former owners or other whites after the war. Attempts by the Freedmen's Bureau to distribute the abandoned lands which Congress placed under its jurisdiction failed when Johnson decided to return those properties to pardoned Confederates. The Southern Homestead Act, passed in February 1866, provided for the sale of remaining federal land; nearly 50 million acres as homesteads. Most of it was timbered, swampy, or poorly drained, and lack of capital prevented most freedmen from homesteading that. Congress defeated every attempt by freedmen to claim reparations in cash payments from the government in consideration of their slave labor.[18]

In view of the generally poor wages and the miserable working conditions imposed upon white workingmen in the North by white businessmen and politicians, it is easy to understand why Congress did not seriously consider the expropriation of property to be transferred to blacks or the payment of cash reparations. Some poor white farmers were just as economically deprived. Blacks successfully contributed to Northern victory in the war, but Northern capitalists were no more concerned to improve the lives of blacks than they were concerned to improve the lives of their own white workers. White workers generally worked long and hard for as little pay as the owner chose to distribute. Working hours, even for children, lasted as long as daylight permitted, and upward mobility was largely a figment of the imagination. In providing the unskilled labor necessary for industrialization the massive immigration of German and Irish peasants deepened the gulf between classes. The Northern wage slave had his conditions of life circumscribed and had no one to take responsibility for him in infancy, old age, illness, or injury, and he was often clothed, housed, and fed little better than a slave. There was no reason to expect the businessmen and politicians who mouthed the rhetoric of opportunity and the work ethic while they exploited white laborers to be concerned to improve the economic conditions of life for blacks.[19]

Most white laborers on the farm or in industry had little to offer blacks even if they had overcome their prejudice in the interest of an alliance between black and white workers. Blacks fared somewhat better when it came to education. Enough philanthropists believed that providing education would not undermine their self-reliance even if reparations or land would. Additionally, by controlling the emphasis of education whites could, in part, control the destiny of the race. Freedmen's aid societies, black and white, and the churches as well as the Freedmen's Bureau helped to establish schools. The private colleges were connected with churches, and providing education was part of proselytization. The schools were as good and prestigious as their backers.[20] When military reconstruction came in 1867, the new constitutions provided for public education.

A number of black men, those in particular who already had some economic wherewithal and education, led the demands for political rights. While encouraging enlistments in 1861, Frederick Douglass explained to blacks that "you have hitherto expressed in various ways not only your willingness but your earnest desire to fulfill any and every obligation which the relationship of citizenship imposes," and military service was one such obligation. Blacks should also enlist in order to learn the art and ability of defense. Furthermore, he asserted, "He who fights the battles of America may claim America as his country and have that claim respected."[21]

As the war dragged on and black soldiers proved their mettle in successfully aiding Union victory, black servicemen expressed similar views of the meaning of such service. The *New Orleans Tribune* on September 6, 1864, declared that the war had brought freedom and the recognition of black manhood, which the black troops "are now fighting valiantly nay heroically to maintain." When James H. Ingraham, a black officer in one of the Native Guard Regiments, appeared at the 1864 National Convention of Colored Men in Syracuse, New York, all business stopped, and he was escorted to the speaker's platform while the delegates stood and cheered. Ingraham told the delegates that despite oppression black men were willing to fight. "This example of magnanimity and patriotism," he declared, "finds no parallel in the world's history." Clearly such service would support a claim to equality after the war.[22]

Frederick Douglass, at the same convention, asserted that political equality, suffrage at least, should be granted after the war. He knew that whites had previously opposed claims to the vote in part because blacks were not required to perform military duty. "Of course this was only a plausible excuse; for we were subject to any call the Government was pleased to make upon us, and we could not properly be made to suffer because the Government did not see fit to impose military duty upon us. The fault was with the Government not with us. Now this frivolous though decent apology for excluding us from the ballot box is entirely swept away." He knew that it could be argued that blacks went into the service without promise of a political reward, but "the fact that, when called into the service of the country, we went forward without exacting terms or conditions, to the mind of the generous man enhances our claims." Even abolitionists asked "why blacks could not be satisfied with personal freedom, the right to testify in courts of law, the right to own, buy and sell real estate, the right to sue and be sued...." Douglass's answer was that "in a republican country without suffrage all other rights become mere privileges, held at the options of others."[23]

On April 15, 1865, the *New Orleans Black Republican* spoke for many blacks when it declared: "Above all, our devotion to our flag, and our manly conduct must be our last appeal and the ground of our hope." But the pleas of blacks for land, money, and the vote fell largely on nonresponsive ears. After all, land and money were not even given to poor whites, and the vote was not given to immigrant working classes. However, legislation could be enacted, without cost, that would appear to reward the freedmen for service in the war, stabilize conditions during the demobilization of black troops, and offer a basis for maintenance of the social and economic status quo.

Congressmen understood that military necessity had brought them closer to enacting legislation providing at least paper equality for the races in the South. Some radicals knew all along where the path would lead but understood that their fellows had to be dragged step by step. The Democrats understood and opposed the military policy all along, but for many congressman who had not seen it clearly before, the civil rights issue was highlighted.

In the Congress, Democrats and Republicans continued to spar over issues related to the Thirteenth Amendment, the Freedmen's Bureau Bill, and the Civil Rights Bill from December through March and into April 1866. In the House, Farnsworth introduced a resolution on December 13, 1865, which expressed the idea that simple justice demanded that black soldiers be awarded citizenship rights. He theorized that if aliens, traitors, and rebels could maintain citizenship rights, then at least blacks who had served in the military should become citizens. Trumbull, who introduced the Civil Rights Act of 1866, favored a distinction between civil rights and political rights. He meant to include the right to come and go, make contracts, rent and lease property, and the like; he did not mean the right to vote. The time was not right, and necessity did not yet in 1866 compel facing the issue. Democrats, like Sydenham E. Ancona of Pennsylvania and John W. Chanler of New York, in the House, and Saulsbury in the Senate, over and over in December made clear their understanding that the second section of the Thirteenth Amendment did not mean giving civil, and certainly not political, rights to blacks.[24]

In January 1866 when Congress considered the bill to grant suffrage to blacks in the District of Columbia, the same issue came up, and the lines were drawn in the same fashion. Republican James F. Wilson of Iowa argued that suffrage was a reward for blacks who gave their all to aid "the nation which had been so cruel to them." Benjamin Boyer, Pennsylvania Democrat, responded that blacks did not need to be rewarded further for military service; they had been rewarded with emancipation. If they were unfit to vote before the war they were still unfit. To educate them and make sure contracts were enforced and labor and property protected as in the Civil Rights Bill, was enough. But Scofield, who favored suffrage, pointed directly to the problem. What could be done with the blacks? Colonization was ridiculous. "If colonization is found impraticable will you try to reenslave them?" He did not think that would work: "the blacks are now too intelligent, too self-reliant and too spirited to submit again to oppression." Andrew J. Rogers, the New Jersey Democrat, however, took a different tack. He disagreed with the policy of awarding suffrage because, logically, women who were citizens, and in some cases had aided in the war effort, would also have to be given the right to vote. He was sure that the Congress agreed with him in opposing suffrage for women. Chanler, in a long speech on January 12, reminded the House that at the beginning of the war "the claim to all the privileges of an American citizen was easily to be foreseen as a consequence of the policy that made the Negro a soldier . . . ." They should not have enlisted blacks in the first place, and he "for one would deny that any obligation rests against this government to do anything more for the Negro than has already been done." Chanler's views did not prevail. On January 30, 1866, Howard told the Senate that "having employed this class of persons to the number of nearly two hundred thousand" the nation would "reap the fruits of our treachery and imbecility in woes which we have not yet witnessed," even worse than the Civil War itself, if legal civil rights protection was not provided.[25]

The majority in Congress of both parties rejected suffrage for blacks but adopted Trumbull's posture of civil rights protection to remove "badges of servitude made in the interest of slavery and as part of slavery."[26] They understood that black consciousness added to the desire of whites in the North to prevent a migration of blacks out of the South, and the continuing objection of some Republicans as far back as 1862 that the government could not use black soldiers and attempt to reenslave them made civil paper equality the absolutely minimum condition of a permanent peace. They enacted the Civil Rights Act of 1866, which guaranteed civil equality to blacks under state law as a response to the need to resolve the race question. If a black person experienced discrimination under state law he could bring a case to federal court. The protection of rights required case by case litigation.[27]

Responses to the enactment of the Civil Rights Act of 1866 came very quickly. In Norfolk, Virginia, on April 16, black citizens gathered outside of town to celebrate with a parade and speeches. White hecklers appeared, and a scuffle broke out. When informed that a white man had been killed, the mayor of the city quickly advised the army that his police force could not cope with the disorder and asked for federal troops, including black soldiers, to keep order. As white Southerners expressed their antipathy toward the congressional enactment, large numbers of blacks were murdered and attacked in the summer of 1866. There were riots in Memphis stimulated when the black Third Regiment of Artillery, which had been keeping order in the city, was mustered out on April 30, 1866. Some of the soldiers kept their weapons upon their discharge. As they celebrated, police arrested two boisterous veterans, but a group of their comrades blocked the way to the police station. Police fired, the veterans fired back and a riot broke out. Whites roamed black neighborhoods, setting fires to churches and schools and beating resisters; the police formed the core of the mob. Finally a new force of federal troops came in to suppress the disturbance.[28]

The Fourteenth Amendment enacted by Congress in June 1866 was designed to resolve any doubts concerning the constitutionality of the Civil Rights Act of 1866, and to make the approach that the protection of the rights of freedom was left primarily a responsibility of state governments, a part of fundamental law. Unlike the Civil Rights Act's positive statement of individual black rights, its provisions were stated negatively. It said that no *state* could interfere with civil rights of persons, not that certain civil rights *belonged* to individuals.

By the end of 1866 and even before the Fourteenth Amendment was ratified, the case litigation approach of the Civil Rights Act was recognized as a failure by a majority in Congress. Southern recalcitrance, the enforcement of Black Codes, pogromlike race riots in Southern cities, including disturbances involving black soldiers, offered visible evidence of white Southern intentions to maintain the status quo ante bellum. In the midst of the open break between President Andrew Johnson and Congress, the will of the Northern majority—that the Republican Party prosper and that the South not be readmitted on a representation basis guaranteeing the resurgence of the slave power by manipulating black voters—required the enactment of Military Reconstruction, including a guarantee of black suffrage, as the next legal step in guaranteeing a permanent rearrangement of power relationships in the South. In terms of legality and constitutional traditions, suffrage seemed to be an appropriate solution. Articulate blacks demanded suffrage, so that now, arguably, they could protect themselves against white oppression and state and local governmental inequities by voting. Many blacks, particularly those from the literate free community before the war, demanded suffrage and the right to hold office as their just due as veterans of the war.[29]

Congress provided suffrage in the Military Reconstruction Act as a means of perpetuating Republican power and out of recognition that reliance on the Fourteenth Amendment alone would require continued national intervention to protect the rights of blacks. The time gained from December 1865 to March 2, 1867, had made it possible to phase out the black soldier problem, to reduce the tension among the black masses, and to impose the old racial order. By 1867, the threat that black soldiers might engage in violent attacks upon whites seemed to be largely erased. However, the lesson of Military Reconstruction was that even when blacks were given suffrage, military protection would be required to prevent white Southerners from overthrowing the radical governments in which blacks participated. The Fifteenth Amendment enacted in February 1869 was a last gasp effort to reconcile the Congressional belief that some assertion of the right of suffrage for blacks should be made fundamental law with the reluctance to interfere directly in state activities. The Fifteenth Amendment was declaratory: it did not require action, military or otherwise, on the part of the national government.[30]

Even before the Fifteenth Amendment was passed it became clear that Republican ascendancy in the presidency could be maintained without blacks if the South was left to become Democratic and the North and East remained Republican. Also, blacks (including war veterans in South Carolina and Louisiana, where they had gained some share in power) themselves agreed with their Northern Republican supporters and extended the olive branch and supported suffrage for white Southerners. The Republican dilemma was resolved; redemption could proceed. Legal and moral responsibilities had been met; suffrage and equality had been enacted into governmental law. Militarily, Black Reconstruction started to become unglued almost as soon as it came into existence. Northern holders of power did not include in their plans a long-term use of soldiers to protect blacks in the South. Even the few local "Negro" militia units, composed of whites and blacks and organized under the Act of March 2, 1867, which struck the word *white* from recruiting regulations of the peacetime federal militia, formed by some of the Republican state governments in 1868, proved ineffective. Radical governors did not use these militia units to protect Unionists from white terrorists as extensively as they should have because of their fears of race war between blacks and whites. In some states, warring factions of Republican politicians used the militia units to engage in warfare against their Republican opponents. White vigilante bands, including the Ku Klux Klan, systematically murdered and intimidated members of the militia groups. Black regular soldiers, long since mustered out, disarmed, or transferred to the frontier, their leavening power among the masses now spent, saw the bright promises of equality come to an end. Military necessity brought blacks into the service, and their efforts helped to win the war and gained the enactment of constitutional amendments and civil rights laws. The war was over, Republican party dominance in national politics was assured, and the economic organization of land, capital, and labor proceeded, North and South, on conventional capitalistic terms. Black people possessed a number of individual freedoms including freedom to worship, attend school, marry and divorce, and have children.[31] Military necessity receded, and even the civil rights laws enacted in its wake soon became so many dead letters, paper things, largely unenforced.

## CHAPTER EIGHT

# IMPLICATIONS FOR THE FUTURE

In the colonial period the issue of whether and how blacks should be used militarily appeared easy to resolve. American colonists placed principal reliance on the British military establishment to defend them from their enemies. The intellectual baggage that the colonists brought to America with them included the European view of militia service as a responsibility as well as a badge of citizenship. Blacks would not be permitted or expected to serve if they were not citizens. If not expected or permitted to serve, that was another indication that they were not citizens. Additionally, if blacks were slaves, there were obvious dangers involved in permitting them to possess arms. At first, when the peril was greatest, blacks were used as extensively as possible. Some colonists objected that blacks could not be trusted and that military service was inconsistent with their status and would interfere with their labor. Only when the colonies became more firmly implanted and warfare decreased did the arguments against using blacks prevail. Blacks, excluded from military duty, were still placed on the lists for emergency service.

During the Revolutionary War blacks fought in the first battles without restriction. In the disorganized state of affairs and in the midst of immediate peril, no one bothered to insist upon exclusion based on their inferior legal status or the possible consequences. As the immediate crisis passed, Southerners, who were never free from their fears of the prospect of insurrection by armed blacks, protested against their inclusion. Most places in the South forbade the bearing of arms by blacks and even the exigencies of war did not permit a general relaxation of the principle. The Continental Congress decided to retain those blacks already in the army, but to exclude all others. In spite of the prohibition, some colonies, more persuaded by need than racial policy and legal consideration, continued to enlist blacks. The British Army began recruiting blacks actively, promising freedom to slave soldiers who enlisted. In Louisiana, where manpower shortages had always been an immediate problem, blacks, long used to military service without regard to the issue of legal status, fought against the British in West Florida in the army of Don Bernardo de Galvez.

The American Revolution resulted immediately in some social reform. Among other manifestations of this development, a slight improvement in the legal status of some blacks occurred. Military necessity compelled some use of black soldiers, and some slave soldiers received their freedom for service in the war. Some Northern states abolished slavery, and the Northwest Ordinance forbade the existence of slavery in the territories. The presence of a few blacks in the army could not provide a basis for improving the condition of blacks in all areas of the country. The war could be, and was, won without the necessity for a large-scale use of black troops; therefore only limited changes occurred. Revolutionary ideology and prerevolutionary antislavery activity, unfettered by the presence of large numbers of blacks, made limited abolition possible in those states where the institution was of lesser economic importance. The few scattered black troops made free and given training in the North did not threaten the maintenance of the institution in the South. Nationally, the Articles of Confederation institutionalized slavery during the war.

Once the war was won, a constitution for the Republic protecting slavery was adopted. In addition to the Three-Fifths Clause and Fugitive Slave Clause, the Constitution made it the duty of the national government to use military force to put down slave insurrection if it occurred. In conformity with the position of constitutional protection of slavery and national responsibility for it, the Congress passed a statute restricting service in the militia to white males. The new Constitution gave control of the militia to the states, but Congress could make laws providing for uniformity in its organization and administration. A statute passed at about the same time providing for regular army enlistment had no racial clause. This development might at first glance seem inconsistent or evidence of enlightened racial views. However, the framers of the laws accepted a distinction between militia duty as the first line of defense and the regular or standing army as volunteer forces whose numbers could be augmented by almost any means necessary in time of war. They recognized the regular army or navy as a place for undesirables who could be drawn from any available source in time of crisis. The militia was both a social and military organization, serving during peacetime as a home guard and a mechanism for slave control where slavery existed. Every able-bodied male citizen was required to serve in it; blacks were *not* citizens and did not have the potential for citizenship. Not every able-bodied male citizen was required to serve in the regular forces, and such service was not a badge of citizenship. The concept of militia duty would have been distorted by including blacks; similarly, the concept of regular service would have been distorted by imposing racial or class restrictions in its manpower utilization. Those states which had not already done so passed militia laws excluding blacks, free and slave, to conform to the federal statute. The racial clause was not removed from the national militia law until July 1862. By that time the need to win a civil war replaced the need to suppress slave insurrections. That war created the conditions in which the issue of the legal status of blacks could be resolved. Including blacks in the militia was one step involved in moving toward abolition and civil rights status for blacks generally.

In the period between 1792 and 1862, only in Louisiana did the law permit the general service of blacks in the militia. Even after the transfer of Louisiana from France to the United States in 1803, Louisiana free Negroes continued to insist on the right to serve in the militia. They had maintained a quasi-free status all during the French and Spanish periods in Louisiana and regarded military service as one indication of their status at a level always slightly higher than that of slaves. The new American government, having agreed to maintain existing rights to the inhabitants in the Louisiana Purchase agreement, permitted free blacks to continue to serve in the militia. They fought in Andrew Jackson's army at the Battle of New Orleans and received commendation for their courageous service.

The brightest hope for an explicit provision for the enlistment of large numbers of blacks and a concomitant improvement in legal status occurred during the War of 1812. The burning of Washington and the continued successes of the British in 1814 compelled the War Department to recommend the adoption of conscription. Congress debated the subject for almost a year but refused to pass a compulsory draft law. Most Americans associated conscription with visions of mercenary and convict armies. During the debate over conscription, Northerners suggested that quotas should be based on total population including slaves. Southern congressmen objected, of course, because they would receive requisitions for larger numbers of men than if only white men were counted, and they had no intention of supplying blacks to fill the quotas. If conscription had been adopted, perhaps, Northern legislators would have pressed the issue. After all, blacks were represented in the Congress, so there was no reason why they should not be counted in draft quotas.

In the War of 1812 and the Mexican War, a few blacks saw military service. Since the statutes regarding the regular army and navy did not exclude them, they were accepted as volunteers when the exigencies of battle were especially pressing. Their numbers, except in the case of

Louisiana, were neither large nor significant enough to compel widespread use of blacks and a thorough revision of the law of slavery and noncitizenship status for blacks. When the Civil War began, military policy did not permit the enlistment of blacks in the service. Most states prohibited the possession of arms by blacks, slave or free, in order to prevent insurrection or rebellion. The general enrollment of blacks in the militia was prohibited in all states except Louisiana, and the National Militia Act of 1792 restricting service to whites was still in force. In the *Dred Scott* case, the Supreme Court affirmed the noncitizenship status of blacks and the recognition of militia duty as a badge of citizenship. Some states provided for the limited service of blacks as hatchetmen, pioneers, and musicians. Occasionally a few free blacks had been accepted into the regular army in emergencies. There were 488,070 free people of color in all the states and territories, and many of them were in Louisiana, where they could serve in the militia. The War Department policy prevented military service by blacks, whether in the militia or the regular army, unless it was absolutely necessary.

Strictly as a war measure, on July 17, 1862, the Congress passed the Second Confiscation Act and the Militia Act. Under these acts, the president could use blacks in the militia. Congress and the president adopted this policy because of the requirements of the war effort and the obvious availability of black manpower. Some volunteer black regiments were organized, under the regular army act, but the number was too small to be of much significance in the Union war effort. The Lincoln administration hesitated to make an all-out effort to recruit blacks. The problem was compounded by the fact that most blacks were slaves. The administration still attempted to squelch Confederate sentiments in the border slave states. Many border state citizens owned slaves, and they opposed projects which would arm blacks or alter the condition of blacks in any way. Lincoln skillfully balanced the opposing interests involved. Some abolitionists saw military service as a means to the end of abolishing slavery and improving the legal status of blacks; some military men needed extra troops and saw no reason why blacks should not be used; some slaveholders opposed the whole project out of self-interest; some politicians thought that black enlistment would violate states' rights as enshrined in the Tenth Amendment of the Constitution. The *Dred Scott* decision, recognizing the noncitizenship of blacks, implied that if blacks were used as soldiers, the issue of citizenship would require resolution.

The greatest single force in the movement to employ black soldiers was the adoption in March 1863 of national conscription. The failure of the volunteer and militia system to provide enough men to prosecute the war forced the federal government to provide for compulsory service.

Now, rather than inclusion in the classes subject to military service, inclusion in the classes of persons subject to the draft became a badge of citizenship. Fulfilling manpower needs resulted in a final blurring of the distinction between the categories of services and large-scale use of traditionally undesirable men. Conscription failed, if one counts only the numbers of men actually inducted. But conscription induced large numbers of men to volunteer. Few white men wanted to be recognized as conscripts. When Congress passed the Conscription Act, it included no racial restrictions in its provisions. When everyone was subjected to compulsory service, blacks could not be exempted. Military necessity, greater now than ever before, compelled a step discussed during the War of 1812 but not taken.

In the summer of 1863, during the first national draft, a great public demand for black troops became evident. Black military service was not just to be permitted but required. Workingmen in the North, who feared economic competition from blacks demanded that blacks be drafted first. Those persons who were opposed to the war and were lukewarm about its prosecution insisted that whenever possible blacks be conscripted instead of white men. Abolitionists welcomed the opportunity to recruit large numbers of blacks. They believed the road to the draft led to abolition and citizenship status for blacks.

In 1864 persons who still doubted the legality of the enlistment of blacks could be bypassed or denounced as unpatriotic. An amendment to the Conscription Act of February 28, 1864, explicitly provided for the enrollment of blacks. Attorney General Edward Bates declared in April 1864 that no prohibition, constitutional or statutory, ever existed regarding the inclusion of blacks in the regular military service. The threshold issue was settled. Blacks were subject to militia duty and they were a part of the national forces. Black males were men. They, too, received the protection of the national government and were expected to aid in its defense. When blacks were obligated to perform military service, their claims to the privilege of citizenship gained momentum and credibility.

With the legalization of black militia and regular army service, the legal walls against abolition gradually came tumbling down. Congress resolved the issues of pay equalization and freedom for the families of slave soldiers on the side of equality, after long struggles and debates over contutionality and states' rights. Continuing military necessity in a long drawn out war made attempts to take the road back to legal slavery impossible. By 1865, abolition was a foregone conclusion. Many Republican politicians believed that black soldiers armed and tempered in battle would not resubmit to slavery without violence, and that they acted as a leaven among the black masses who shared their staunch defense of freedom. Passing the Thirteenth Amendment gave slavery's opponents the opportunity to cut themselves loose from a dead issue.

The black soldier problem did not go away once the war was over. During the long process of muster-out black soldiers at times outnumbered white soldiers in some counties in the South. White Southerners, Union Army generals, and politicians became concerned about the threatening presence of black soldiers and black veterans in the South, particularly as white troops demanded rapid muster-out. Additionally, whites in the North did not want to stimulate a great influx of black men, women, and children into their midst. The Congress searched for some legal way to settle the peacetime status of blacks. They desired a solution within the framework of black aspirations, white self-interest, and generally accepted constitutional theory. They enacted the Civil Rights Act of 1866, which gave much the same legal status at least on paper in the North and the South.

The Civil Rights Act of 1866, based on the authority of the Thirteenth Amendment, was a conservative constitutional response to the need to resolve the race question. Blacks received citizenship status and equal civil rights under state law, but not the right to vote. If a black person claimed discrimination under state law, he could bring a case in federal court in order to enforce his rights. Enforcement required case-by-case litigation. On the basis of this paper civil equality, Reconstruction proceeded under a new legal order.

By the end of 1866, a majority in Congress as well as the black population and their white allies recognized the failure of the case litigation method and the Civil Rights Act of 1866. The Southerners reconstructed the old politics in their section and enacted some of the worst legal features of slavery. If the South was not to be readmitted to the Union on a representation basis that would guarantee the resurgence of the slave power—on the backs of blacks—some other measure had to be tried. Black spokesmen, including black soldiers and veterans, demanded the right to vote and hold office. Congress insisted on Military Reconstruction and the ratification of the Fourteenth Amendment as the next proposed solutions. Equal rights without suffrage had not worked; now it would be equal rights with suffrage. The Fourteenth Amendment, which was passed in both houses of Congress in its final form on June 13, 1866, evolved from the conditions created by the enlistment of blacks in the service, which had led to emancipation and the enactment of the Thirteenth Amendment.

Military Reconstruction, too, was a partial failure. Some blacks, particularly in Louisiana and South Carolina, including black veterans, experienced the pleasures and duties of holding political office. Northern whites, who had their own internal political problems, did not believe it was right or necessary to maintain military control in the South or to permit the institutionalization of real black participation in government. Besides, Republican control of the presidency and patronage could be maintained even if the South went completely Democratic. Black soldiers had by that time been transferred to the frontier or long since demobilized and largely disarmed. No military necessity stood in the way of redemption. The enactment of the Fifteenth Amendment in April 1869, an indirect result of emancipation, was the final Reconstruction effort to provide a political solution to the changed race relations evolving from the war. The necessity for using black soldiers to insure Union victory led directly not only to abolition but to the enactment of the Civil Rights Act of 1866 and the Fourteenth Amendment; indirectly it led to the enactment of the Fifteenth Amendment. But necessity had receded, the laws once enacted became dead letters, and the conditions of black life and the organization of black labor remained largely the same. The six permanent black army regiments organized by Congress in 1866 were stationed west of the Mississippi on the frontier. Until some other necessity, military or otherwise, moved the levers of power, new constitutional and legal devices to advance the cause of racial equality would not be attempted.

In addition to other factors, a correlation between the improvement (or lack thereof) in the legal status of blacks and military necessity may be perceived in the period since Reconstruction. Although in the Indian wars, Spanish American War, and World War I black troops played a large and conspicuous part in some of the major campaigns, the holders of power did not regard the use of black manpower as absolutely essential for victory. No improvement in legal status resulted. In fact, the civil rights laws already enacted remained unenforced, and discrimination was the rule and not the exception in the aftermath of those wars. When World War I was still in progress and one-third of the total American army were blacks, ninety-six blacks were lynched in 1917 and 1918. The Ku Klux Klan rearmed in 1915 and began its growth as a national organization in the early 1920's.

In World War II the characteristics of the enemy—the racism of the Nazis on the one hand and the fear that blacks might support the Japanese who were people of color on the other—as well as the requirements for the war itself abroad and on the homefront, created an environment in which slight improvement in the legal status of blacks could and did occur. The Korean War ensued in the general environment of slight progress engendered during World War II. The war in Vietnam presented the interesting phenomenon of an army comprised of disproportionately large numbers of blacks not only fighting but being required to assist in controlling civil rights disturbances and rebellions of blacks and their white allies. In the twentieth century the relationship observed in the military case might best be discussed in the context of other crises—for example, economic dislocations in an international setting or the struggle for political and economic dominance by the United States and its allies against Russian and Chinese interests in the less-developed countries. In any case, the civil rights measures of the First Reconstruction evolved, in part, from traditional notions of military enlistment policy and citizenship status that had developed in the antebellum period. Based on the antebellum and Civil War experiences, if the resolution of a military or other crisis should dictate egalitarian racial policy solutions, the law will be interpreted to permit such solutions, or the Constitution will be amended.

# NOTES

### EPIGRAPH

*Dred Scott* v. *Sandford*, 19 Howard 393 (1857), p. 415.

### CHAPTER ONE

1. David Brion Davis, *The Problem of Slavery in Western Culture* (Ithaca, New York, 1966), pp. 31, 58; Winthrop Jordan, *White over Black: American Attitudes Toward the Negro* (Chapel Hill, 1968).
2. Lindsay Boynton, *The Elizabethan Militia, 1588-1638* (London, 1967); Charles W. Hollister, *Anglo-Saxon Military Institutions on the Eve of the Norman Conquest* (Oxford, 1962); Michael Powicke, *Military Obligations in Medieval England, A Study in Liberty and Duty* (Oxford, 1962); John R. Western, *The English Militia in the Eighteenth Century: The Story of a Political Issue, 1660-1802* (London, 1965), p. 455.
3. Morrison Sharp, "Leadership and Democracy in the Early New England System of Defense," *American Historical Review* 50 (1944), 244-60; John W. Shy, "A New Look at Colonial Militia," *William and Mary Quarterly* 20 (1963), 175-85; Ronald L. Boucher, "The Colonial Militia as a Social Institution: Salem, Massachusetts 1764-75," *Military Affairs* (1973), 125-29. In the British Parliament, views were expressed as late as the 1750's that the colonial army contained some of the better people. In debate on whether the punishment provision of the Mutiny Bill should be extended to Americans, Robert Viner opposed the extension because, unlike British regiments composed of "the very lowest and most abandoned of our people," the American soldiers were the "gentlemen, freeholders, farmers and master tradesmen of the country . . . It was of such men that our armies of old chiefly consisted. . . ." William Cobbett, ed. *The Parliamentary History*

*of England from the Earliest Period to the Year 1803* (36 vols., London, 1813), vol. 36, pp. 376-78.

4. Davis, *Slavery in Western Culture,* pp. 50-52, 59, 138..

5. *The Records of the Governor and Company of Massachusetts Bay in New England, 1628-1686* (5 vols., Boston, 1853-55), vol. 2, p. 268; vol. 3, p. 397; Lorenzo J. Greene, *The Negro in Colonial New England* (New York, 1942; reprinted, Atheneum, 1969), pp. 126-28.

6. Donald Robinson, *Slavery in the Structure of American Politics, 1765-1820* (New York, 1971), pp. 18-20.

7. *Acts and Laws Passed by the Great and General Court of the Massachusetts Bay in New England from 1692-1719* (London, 1724), pp. 48, 221, 242; Benjamin Quarles, "The Colonial Militia and Negro Manpower," *Mississippi Valley Historical Review* 45 (1959), 513-21; Robert Twombly and Robert Moore, "Black Puritan: The Negro in Seventeenth Century Massachusetts," *William and Mary Quarterly* 24 (1967), 224-421.

8. John Hope Franklin, *From Slavery to Freedom* (New York, 1967), pp. 89-99; Edgar J. McManus, *Black Bondage in the North* (New York, 1973), pp. 70-71.

9. *The Statutes at Large of South Carolina, 1682-1871* (14 vols., Columbia, 1836-72), vol. 9, pp. 658-61, 680; Shy, "New Look at Colonial Militia," p. 181; Mary F. Berry, *Black Resistance/White Law : A History of Constitutional Racism in America* (New York, 1971), pp. 2-3.

10. Marcelin De Fourneaux, *Daily Life in Spain in the Golden Age* (New York, 1971), pp. 207-8; David W. Cohen and Jack P. Greene, eds., *Neither Slave Nor Free: The Freedmen of African Descent in the Slave Societies of the New World* (Baltimore, 1972), pp. 10, 15-16; 39-44; 69, 109, 113, 117, 120-29; 136, 175, 197-9; 208.

11. Charles Etienne Gayarre, *History of Louisiana* (4 vols., New Orleans, 1830-31), vol. 1. pp. 242, 254, 366, 454; Roland C. McConnell, *Negro Troops of Ante-Bellum Louisiana* (Baton Rouge, 1968), pp. 4-5.

12. Dumont de Montigny, *Memoires Historiques Sur La Louisiane* (Paris, 1753), pp. 225-26; Mc Connell, *Negro Troops,* pp. 6-7, 10-11.

13. Henry Dart, "Index to the Spanish Judicial Records," *Louisiana Historical Quarterly* 6 (1923), passim; in recent articles A. E. Keir Nash and Daniel Flanigan have described appellate court responses in a few trials involving blacks in the South. The cases involve capital crimes and are of nineteenth-century vintage. See A. E. Keir Nash, "Negro Rights, Unionism, and Greatness on the South Carolina Court of Appeals: The Extraordinary Chief Justice John Belton O'Neall," *South Carolina Law Review* 21 (1969), 141-90; "A More Equitable Past? Southern Supreme Courts and the Protection of the Antebellum Negro," *North Carolina Law Review* 48 (1969), 197-242; "Fairness and Formalism in the Trials of Blacks in the State Supreme Courts of the Old South," *Virginia Law Review* 56 (Feb. 1970), 64-100; "The Texas Supreme Court and Trial Rights of Blacks, 1845-1860," *Journal of American History* 58 (Dec. 1971), 622-42; Daniel Flanigan, "Criminal Procedure in Slave Trials in the Antebellum South," *Journal of Southern History* 40 (1972), 537-64.

14. John W. Caughey, *Bernado de Galvez in Louisiana, 1776-1783* (Berke-

ley, 1934), p. 41; McConnell, *Negro Troops*, p. 17.

15. Bernard Bailyn, *The Ideological Origins of the American Revolution* (Cambridge, 1967), p. 162; Davis, *The Problem of Slavery in Western Culture*, pp. 142, 411-421; 427-33; see also Samuel Sewall, *The Selling of Joseph* (Boston, 1700); Benjamin Lay, "Slave-keepers That Keep the Innocent in Bondage, Apostates . . . " (Philadelphia, 1737); Lawrence W. Towner, "The Sewall-Saffin Dialogue on Slavery," *William and Mary Quarterly*, 3rd ser., vol. 21 (1964), 40-52; Leonard W. Labaree, ed., *The Papers of Benjamin Franklin* (New York, 1941), p. 216; Bernard Bailyn, ed. *Pamphlets of the American Revolution, 1750-1776* (Cambridge, 1965), vol. 1, pp. 438-40, 409, 446.

16. *Journals of the Continental Congress* vol. 6, pp. 1102-6, 1079-82; Edmund Burnett, ed., *Letters of Members of the Continental Congress* (8 vols., Washington, 1921-36), vol. 2, p. 564; Robinson, *Slavery in the Structure of American Politics*, pp. 148-49.

17. *Journals of the Continental Congress*, vol. 9, pp. 637-40, 647-56; Article II, Articles of Confederation.

18. Evarts B. Greene and Virginia D. Harrington, *American Population Before the Federal Census of 1790* (New York, 1932), pp. 141-2, 177-79; *Massachusetts Soldiers and Sailors in the Revolutionary War* (17 vols., Boston, 1896-1908), vol. 12, p. 743; Benjamin Quarles, *The Negro in the American Revolution* (Chapel Hill, 1961), pp. 9-10.

19. *Journals of the Continental Congress*, vol. 2, p. 89.

20. John Adams, *Works*, ed. Charles Francis Adams (10 vols., Boston, 1850-56), vol. 2, pp. 417-18.

21. *Massachusetts Soldiers and Sailors in the Revolutionary War*, vol. 13, p. 743; vol. 9, p. 725; Benjamin Quarles, *Negro in the American Revolution*, pp. 10-12.

22. *Journals of the Continental Congress*, vol. 2, pp. 221, vol. 3, p. 188.

23. Peter Force, ed. *American Archives*, in *Documentary History of . . . the North American Colonies*, 4th ser. (6 vols., Washington, 1837-53), vol. 3, p. 1385; Frank Moore, *Diary of the American Revolution* (2 vols., New York, 1865), vol. 1, p. 110; Quarles, *Negro in the American Revolution*, p. 15.

24. Adams, *Works*, vol. 2, p. 422; *Journals of the Continental Congress*, vol. 3, p. 263; "Diary of Richard Smith in the Continental Congress, 1775-1776," *American Historical Review* 1 (1895), 292; Quarles, *Negro in the American Revolution*, pp. 15-16; The Journals do not report the number of votes on Rutledge's motion.

25. John Fitzpatrick, ed., *The Writings of George Washington* (30 vols., Washington, 1931-34), vol. 4, p. 8; Force, *American Archives . . .* vol. 4, p. 1161; "The Orderly Books of Colonel William Hearnshaw," *American Antiquarian Society Proceedings* 57 (1947), 32; Quarles, *Negro in the American Revolution*, pp. 15-16.

26. *Journals of the Continental Congress*, vol. 4, p. 60; Quarles, *Negro in the American Revolution*, pp. 16, 19-32; the Proclamation is in Force, *American Archives*, vol. 3, pp. 1385, 1011; Robinson, *Slavery in the Structure of American Politics*, pp. 104-15 and notes there cited on British reluctance.

27. *Acts and Resolves Public and Private of the Province of Massachusetts Bay*, (14 vols., Boston, 1868–70), vol. 5, pp. 445, 451; also see, for

example, *The Statutes at Large of South Carolina*, vol. 9, p. 680; New York, *Laws of the State*, 1st session, p. 31 (Poughkeepsie, 1922).

28. Edward Tatum, ed., *The American Journal of Ambrose Serle, Secretary to Lord Howe, 1776-1778* (San Marino, Calif., 1940), p. 880.
29. Adams, *Works*, vol. 3, p. 48; Quarles, *Negro in the American Revolution*, pp. 53-55.
30. Lorenzo Greene, "Some Observations on the Black Regiment of Rhode Island in the American Revolution," *Journal of Negro History* 37 (1952); *Records of the State of Rhode Island and Providence Plantations in New England* (10 vols., Providence, 1856-65), vol. 8, pp. 359-61.
31. Burnett, *Letters of the Members of the Continental Congress*, vol. 4, p. 107; Fitzpatrick, *Writings of Washington*, vol. 4, p. 267; Richard B. Morris, ed., *Alexander Hamilton and the Founding of the Nation* (New York, 1957), pp. 454-55; Quarles, *Negro in the American Revolution*, pp. 60-62.
32. *Journals of the Continental Congress*, vol. 13, p. 388; Robert W. Gibbes, ed., *Documentary History of the American Revolution* (3 vols., New York, 1883-87), vol. 2, p. 121; Walter Clark, ed., *The State Records of North Carolina* (26 vols., Goldsboro, 1886-1907), vol. 19, pp. 911-14.
33. Jared Sparks, ed., *Correspondence of the American Revolution: Being Letters of Eminent Men to George Washington from the Time of His Taking Command to the End of His Presidency* (4 vols., Boston, 1853), vol. 3, pp. 466-67.
34. Quarles, *Negro in the American Revolution*, pp. 52-54, 56-57, 64-67.
35. Reuben Thwaites and Louise Kellogg, eds., *Frontier Defense on the Upper Ohio, 1778-79* (Madison, Wis., 1912), pp. 1, 226; James A. James, "Spanish Influence in the West During the American Revolution," *Mississippi Valley Historical Review* 4 (1917), 198-99; McConnell, *Free Negro Troops*, pp. 17-18.
36. Thwaites and Kellogg, *Frontier Defense*, p. 91; Burnett, *Letters of Members of the Continental Congress*, vol 2, pp. 446-47.
37. *Journals of the Continental Congress*, vol. 2, p. 91.
38. Jac Nachbin, "Suplemento a la Gazeta de Madrid," English translation, *Louisiana Historical Quarterly*, vol. 15, pp. 468-81; Manuel Serrano Y Sanz, ed., *Documentos Historicos de la Florida y la Louisiana, Siglos XVI and XVIII* (Madrid, 1912), p. 348; McConnell, *Free Negro Troops*, pp. 17-18.
39. Sanz, *Documentos Historicos*, p. 349; Caughey, *Bernardo de Galvez*, pp. 174-75; "Diary of the Operations of the Expedition Against the Place of Pensacola, Conducted by the Armies of H. Catholic M., Under the Orders of the Field Marshal Don Bernardo de Galvez," *Louisiana Historical Quarterly*, 1 (1917), 44-48, 74-75; "Papers from the Canadian Archives, 1778-1783," *Collections of the Wisconsin State Historical Society* 11 (1889), 97-212; McConnell, *Free Negro Troops*, pp. 18-20.
40. Arthur Zilversmit, *The First Emancipation, The Abolition of Slavery in the North* (Chicago, 1967), pp. 226-29; Jordan, *White over Black*, p. 307.

CHAPTER TWO

1. Max Farrand, ed., *Records of the Federal Convention*, (4 vols., New Haven, 1911), vol. 1, pp. 447, 486, vol. 2, p. 10; *Federalist*, nos. 51 and 10; Robinson, *Slavery in the Structure of American Politics*, p. 178.

2. *Journals of the Continental Congress*, vol. 24, p. 293, vol. 25, pp. 948-49, 951-52, vol. 30, p. 106; Robinson, *Slavery in the Structure of American Politics*, pp. 157-60.

3. *American State Papers*, Military Affairs, (7 vols., Washington, 1832-60), vol. 1, pp. 5,6; Farrand, *Records*, vol. 2, pp. 220-22, vol. 3, p. 84; Henry Wilson, *History of the Rise and Fall of the Slave Power in America*, (3 vols., Boston, 1875), vol. 1, pp. 47-48; Ernest M. Lander, "The South Carolinians at the Philadelphia Convention, 1787," *South Carolina Magazine of History* 57 (1956), p. 316; Jonathan Elliot, ed., *The Debates in the Several State Conventions on the Adoption of the Federal Constitution*, 5 vols. (Philadelphia, 1861), vol. 3, pp. 427, 254, 325, vol. 4, pp. 315-16; Marvin R. Zahniser, *Charles Cotesworth Pinckney, Founding Father* (Chapel Hill, 1967), pp. 89-99; Berry, *Black Resistance*, pp. 8-9.

4. The militia organization provision is in Article 1, Section 8, Clause 16 of the Constitution. See also *Houston v. Moore*, 5 Wheat. 1, 16 (1820); Leon Litwack, *North of Slavery: The Negro in the Free States, 1790-1860* (Chicago, 1961), pp. 31-33; Robinson, *Slavery in the Structure of American Politics*, pp. 253-55; *Annals of the Congress of the United States, 1789-1824* (42 vols., Washington, 1834-56), 2nd Congress, 1st session, pp. 418-423, 557, 1040; for information on opinion concerning standing armies, Leon Friedman, "Conscription and the Constitution: The Original Understanding," *Michigan Law Review* (June, 1969), 1493-1552; also J. B. McMaster and F. D. Stone, eds. *Pennsylvania and the Federal Constitution, 1787-1788* (Lancaster, 1885), pp. 151-56, 570, 585, 598; Elliot, vol. 2, pp. 468-554, vol. 4, p. 245; Also *Federalist*, nos. 22,23,25; U.S., *Statutes at Large of the United States, 1789-1869* (15 vols., Boston, 1845-73), vol. 2, pp. 271-77. On the fear of insurrection and Article 4, section 4, the Domestic Violence Clause of the Constitution, see Berry, *Black Resistance*, esp. chaps. 1-3, and Staughton Lynd, *Class Conflict, Slavery and the United States Constitution* (Indianapolis, 1967), pp. 153-54; but c.f. Robinson, *Slavery in the Structure of American Politics*, p. 218.

5. *Massachusetts Laws, 1780-1814* (5 vols., Boston, 1807-15), vol. 3, p. 579; *Annals of Congress*, 8th Congress, 2nd session, pp. 1058-59, 1570.

6. Donald Everett, "Emigres and Militiamen: Free Persons of Color in New Orleans, 1803-18," *Journal of Negro History* 38 (1953), 377-402; McConnell, *Negro Troops*, pp. 33-34; Clarence E. Carter, ed., *Territorial Papers of the United States* (18 vols., Washington, 1934-), vol. 9, p. 59; Dunbar Rowland, ed., *Official Letter Books of W. C. C. Claiborne, 1801-1816* (6 vols., Jackson, Miss., 1917), vol. 2, p. 218. There were one free black company and two of mulattoes.

7. Gayarre, *History of Louisiana*, vol. 2, pp. 219-20.

8. James Robertson, ed., *Louisiana under Spain, France, and the United States* (2 vols., Cleveland, 1911), vol. 2, p. 228.
9. Carter, *Territorial Papers*, vol. 9, p. 174; McConnell, *Negro Troops*, pp. 36-40.
10. Rowland, *Letter Books*, vol. 2, pp. 54-55, 218-19.
11. Louisiana, Territory of New Orleans, *Laws, 1804-05* (New Orleans, 1802), p. 262.
12. Carter, *Territorial Papers*, vol. 9, p. 561.
13. Louisiana, *Laws, 1806-7* (New Orleans, 1808), pp. 188-90.
14. Louisiana, *Laws, 1807-8* (New Orleans, 1809), p. 138.
15. Rowland, *Letter Books*, vol. 5, p. 100, vol. 6, p. 132.
16. *Acts Passed at the First Session of the First General Assembly of the State of Louisiana* (New Orleans, 1812), p. 72.
17. U.S., *Statutes at Large*, vol. 2, pp. 271-77.
18. Emory Upton, *The Military Policy of the United States*, War Department Document No. 290, 1917 (Washington, 1917), p. 123; *Washington Daily National Intelligencer*, September 22, 1814; *Annals of Congress*, 13th Congress, 3rd Session, pp. 12-15; Jack Leach, *Conscription in the United States, Historical Background* (Rutland, Vt., 1952), pp. 31-33.
19. *Annals of Congress*, 13th Congress, 3rd Session, pp. 482-6, 1502; Leach, *Conscription*, pp. 62-64.
20. *Annals of Congress*, 13th Congress, 3rd Session, pp. 800-819, 834-67, 886-98, 928-29; Leach, *Conscription*, pp. 97-98.
21. *Annals of Congress*, 13th Congress, 3rd Session, pp. 800-819, 928-29; Leach, *Conscription*, pp. 97-98.
22. Henry Adams, ed., *Documents Relating to New England Federalism: 1800-1815* (Boston, 1877), p. 403; Samuel E. Morison, *The Life and Letters of Harrison Gray Otis, Federalist: 1765-1818* (2 vols., Boston, 1913), vol. 2, pp. 101-2; James M. Banner, *To the Hartford Convention: The Federalist and the Origins of Party Politics in Massachusetts, 1789-1815* (New York, 1970); Leach, *Conscription*, pp. 104-6.
23. *Annals of Congress*, 13th Congress, 3rd Session, pp. 141, 771, 993-94; Fletcher Webster, ed., *Writings and Speeches of Daniel Webster; Private Correspondence* (18 vols., Boston, 1903), vol. 1, p. 249; Leach, *Conscription*, pp. 78, 117.
24. John S. Bassett, ed., *The Correspondence of Andrew Jackson* (17 vols., Washington, 1926-35), vol. 2, pp. 76-77.
25. Lacarrier Latour, *Historical Memoir of the War in West Florida* (Philadelphia, 1816), pp. 31-32.
26. Rowland, *Letter Books*, vol. 6, p. 294.
27. Bassett, *Correspondence*, vol. 2, pp. 87-88.
28. Rowland, *Letter Books*, vol. 6, pp. 320-21; Bassett *Correspondence*, vol. 2, p. 100.
29. Bassett, "Major Howell Tatum's Journal," *Smith College Studies in History* 7 (1922), 98.
30. Gayarre, *History of Louisiana*, vol. 4, p. 406.
31. *The Negro in the Military Service . . . to 1888*, A Compilation of Official Records . . . , War Department, Record Group 94, MS, National Archives, vol. 3, p. 397.

32. *Acts Passed by the Second Session of the First Legislature of the State of Louisiana* (New Orleans, 1816), p. 102; *Acts Passed by the First Session of the Fourth Legislature of the State of Louisiana* (New Orleans, 1918), p. 10.

33. *New Orleans Daily Picayune*, January 9, 1851; January 9, 1856; January 9, 1859.

34. New York, *Laws of the State*, 38th Session, pp. 22-23; *Washington Daily National Intelligencer*, August 16, 17, November 11, 1814.

35. U.S., *Official Opinions of the Attorneys General of the United States Advising the President and Heads of Departments of Their Official Duties and Expounding the Constitution, Treaties with Foreign Governments and with Indian Tribes, and the Public Laws of the Country* (38 vols., Washington, 1852-), vol. 1, pp. 602-3; Leon Litwack, "The Federal Government and the Free Negro," *Journal of Negro History* 43 (1958), 273; Litwack, *North of Slavery*, p. 33.

36. Litwack, *North of Slavery*, p. 33; *Congressional Globe*, 27th Congress, 2nd Session, pp. 805-7, 3rd Session, p. 174.

37. U.S., *Statutes at Large*, vol. 9, pp. 9-10; Nell, *Colored Patriots*, pp. 296, 313; U.S., *Messages of the President of the United States with the Correspondence Therewith Communicated Between the Secretary of War and Other Officers of the Government, on the Subject of the Mexican War* (Washington, 1848), pp. 935-7.

38. *Official Reports of the Debates and Proceedings in the State Convention to Revise and Amend the Constitution of the Commonwealth of Massachusetts* (8 vols., Boston, 1853), vol. 1, pp. 553-68; William C. Nell, *Colored Patriots of the American Revolution* (Boston, 1855), pp. 101-10; U.S., *Statutes at Large*, vol. 13, p. 731; *Acts and Resolves Passed by the General Court of Massachusetts at the Second Session, 1859* (Boston, 1859), pp. 692-95, 702, 707; James McPherson, *The Struggle for Equality, Abolitionists and the Negro in the Civil War and Reconstruction* (Princeton, 1964), p. 192; *Boston Daily Evening Transcript*; June 21, 1853; *Boston Morning Journal*, June 22, 1853. See also Wendell Phillips, ed., *The Constitution, a Pro-slavery Compact* (New York, 3rd ed., 1956); Stanley B. Bernstein "Abolitionist Readings of the Constitution," Ph.D. dissertation, Harvard University; pp. 149-50; *Liberator*, March 11, 1853, May 13 and July 1, 1853, discussed in Jane H. Pease and William H. Pease, *They Who Would Be Free: Blacks Search For Freedom, 1830-1861* (New York, 1974), pp. 158-59.

39. *Boston Daily Advertiser*, March 2, 13, 14, 16, 1869; *Liberator* March 2, 1860; Pease and Pease, *They Who Would Be Free*, pp. 159-60.

## CHAPTER THREE

1. John Hope Franklin, *The Militant South, 1800-1861* (Cambridge, 1956), pp. 171-73, 176-79.

2. U.S., *Provost Marshal General's Final Report of March 17, 1866*, Executive Document No. 1, (16 vols., Washington, 1866) 39th Congress, 1st session, vol. 1, p. 6; Leach, *Conscription*, pp. 130-31; *Census of the United States, 1860*.

3. Emory Upton, *The Military Policy of the United States*, War Department Document No. 290, 1917 (Washington, 1917), p. 225; *Dred Scot* v. *Sandford*, 19 Howard 393 (1857).
4. U.S., *Provost Marshal General's Final Report*, vol. 1, pp. 6-8; William T. Sherman, *Memoirs of General William T. Sherman* (2 vols., New York, 1875), vol. 2, p. 383; Edward McPherson, *Political History of the United States During the Great Rebellion* (Washington, 1865), pp. 114-15; Leach, *Conscription*, p. 132.
5. U.S., Adjutant General's Office, *Statement of the Number of Men Called by the President of the United States and the Number Furnished from April 15, 1861, to the Close of the War of the Rebellion* (Washington, 1880), pt. 2; U.S., *Provost Marshal General's Final Report*, vol. 2, p. 8; Leach, *Conscription*, p. 132.
6. *New York Times*, April 6, 1861; *Washington Daily National Intelligencer*, May 20, 1861; *Nashville Republican Banner*, May 10, 1861; Dudley Cornish, *The Sable Arm: Negro Troops in the Union Army, 1861-1865* (New York, 1956), pp. 4-7; James McPherson, *The Negro's Civil War: How American Negroes Felt and Acted During the War for the Union* (New York, 1965), pp. 19-23; Benjamin Quarles, *The Negro in the Civil War* (Boston, 1969), pp. 26-30, 453, 184, in which Douglass is quoted; McPherson, *Struggle for Equality*, chapters 3 and 4 passim and esp. pp. 60-61; V. Jacque Voegeli, *Free But Not Equal: The Midwest and the Negro During the Civil War* (Chicago, 1967), pp. 17-20.
7. U.S., War Department, *The War of the Rebellion: A Compilation of the Official Records of the Union and Confederate Armies* (128 vols., Washington, 1880-1901), vol. 3, p. 467, hereafter cited as *O.R.*, John Nicolay and John Hay, *Abraham Lincoln: A History* (10 vols., New York, 1886), vol. 4, pp. 416-20.
8. *Public Acts of the State of Tennessee*, 33rd General Assembly, extra session, chap. 24, pp. 49-50; *The Statutes at Large of South Carolina*, vol. 9, p. 693. Quarles, *Negro in the Civil War*, pp. 36-39; *New Orleans Daily True Delta*, April 23, 27, May 2, 1861, *O.R.*, ser. 1, vol. 15, p. 555; Muster Rolls, First Native Guards, Louisiana Militia, Confederate States of America, May 3, 1861, Record Group 109, War Department Collection of Confederate Group Records, MS, National Archives, hereafter referred to as R.G. 109; John Winters, *The Civil War in Louisiana* (Baton Rouge, 1963), pp. 34-35, incorrectly claims that the officers were not blacks; see Mary F. Berry, "Negro Troops in Blue and Gray: The Louisiana Native Guards, 1861-1863," *Louisiana History* 8 (Spring 1967), 165-90.
9. Eighth Census of the Free Inhabitants of New Orleans (1860), vols. 5-9, MS, National Archives; Muster Rolls, First Native Guards, Confederate States of America, R. G. 109; Quarles, *Negro in the Civil War*, pp. 64-65; Harold Hyman, *A More Perfect Union* (New York, 1973), pp. 64-67; *O.R.*, ser. 1, vol. 52, supplement 746, Major General John Lewis, Commanding, Confederate Militia, State of Louisiana, to New Orleans Militia Headquarters, September 29, 1861.
10. *Congressional Globe* (Washington, 1861-67), 37th Congress, 2nd Session, pp. 1, 16-19, 57-60, 130-31; Cornish, *Sable Arm*, p. 26.
11. U.S., *Provost Marshal General's Final Report*, vol. 2, p. 9; *Final Re-*

*port of the Provost Marshal General on the Operation of the Selective Service System to July 15, 1919* (Washington, 1920), appendix J., p. 369; George E. Baker, ed., *The Works of William H. Seward* (15 vols., Boston, 1884-85), vol. 4, p. 55; Leach, *Conscription*, p. 134.

12. Confederate States of America, *Statutes at Large from the Institution of the Government to February 17, 1864* (2 vols., Richmond, 1862-64), 1st Congress, 1st Session, vol., pp. 29-32; *Journal of the Congress of the Confederate States, 1861-1865*, printed as U.S. Senate Document, 58th Congress, 2nd Session (7 vols., Washington, 1905-6), vol. 2, pp. 114 ff.; Leach, *Conscription*, p. 136. The Confederate statute did not, of course, apply to blacks.

13. Charlotte Forten, "Life on the Sea Islands," *Atlantic Monthly* 13 (May-June 1864), 588-96, 666-76; Cornish, *Sable Arm*, p. 34; Willie Lee Rose, *Rehearsal for Reconstruction: The Port Royal Experiment* (New York, 1964), pp. 21-31.

14. *O.R.*, ser. 1, vol. 14, pp. 333-41; *O.R.*, ser. 3, vol. 2, p. 43. Rose, *Rehearsal*, pp. 144-51.

15. *O.R.*, ser. 1, vol. 2, pp. 50-60, 148, 197; *Washington Daily National Intelligencer*, May 27, 1862, May 30, 1862; Cornish, *Sable Arm* pp. 35-36.

16. U.S., *Provost Marshal General's Final Report*, vol. 1, p. 9; *O.R.*, ser. 3, vol. 3, p. 109, vol. 4, p. 1264; Leach, *Conscription*, p. 137.

17. Frederick W. Seward, *Seward at Washington as Senator and Secretary of State: A Memoir of His Life with Selections from His Letters* (New York, 1891), p. 115; L. D. Ingersoll, *A History of the War Department of the United States* (Washington, 1879), p. 333; Leach, *Conscription*, p. 138.

18. U.S., *Statutes at Large*, vol. 13, pp. 597-600; James G. Randall, *Constitutional Problems under Lincoln* (New York, 1926), pp. 244-47; Leach, *Conscription*, p. 139.

19. *Congressional Globe*, 37th Congress, 2nd Session, pp. 196, 2246, 2264, 2274, 2297-99, 2972, 3087, 3102, 3109, 3121-24, 3198-99; 3rd Session, 3250-51, 3254, 3337-39, 3343, appendix, 415.

20. U.S., *Provost Marshal General's Final Report*, vol. 1, p. 11; vol. 2, pp. 105-7; *O.R.*, ser. 3, vol. 2, pp. 333-35; Leach, *Conscription*.

21. *O.R.*, ser. 3, vol. 2, pp. 370; U.S., *Provost Marshal General's Final Report*, vol. 1, pp. 11-12; Leach, *Conscription*.

22. *O. R.*, ser. 1, vol. 3, p. 516, ser. 3, vol. 2, pp. 294-95, 445; *Washington Daily National Intelligencer*, October 13, 1862; U.S., War Department, *Official Register of the Volunteer Forces of the Army for the Years 1861, 1862, 1863, 1864, 1865* (8 parts, Washington, 1867), pt. 8, pp. 25-26; Cornish, *Sable Arm*, pp. 69-78.

23. John W. Blassingame, *Black New Orleans, 1860-1880* (Chicago, 1973), pp. 30-31, 33, and notes there cited. *New Orleans Tribune*, December 7, 1864; some historians emphasize Butler's fear of blacks' potential for violence as a reason for his decision to impose the "discipline" of military service. Whatever the merits of that interpretation, Butler inducted black soldiers because they were needed. See, for example, William F. Messner, "Black Violence and White Response: Louisiana, 1862," *Journal of Southern History* 41 (February 1965), 19-38.

24. Kate M. Rowland, ed., *The Journal of Julia Le Grand, 1862-1863* (Richmond, 1911), pp. 130, 140; *Douglass' Monthly*, April 1863, p. 829; Recruiting Speech, 1862, P. B. S. Pinchback Papers, Howard University; Albert Stearns and James Bowen, May 28, 1863, K. Fuller to Butler, November 19, 1862, Department of the Gulf, Provost Marshal General, Record Group 393, National Archives; John W. Blassingame, "A Social and Economic Study of the Negro in New Orleans, 1860-1880," Ph.D. dissertation, Yale University 1971, pp. 73-76, and notes there cited.

25. *O.R.*, ser. 1, vol. 14, p. 377, ser. 3, vol. 2, p. 345; Hunter, denied arms and equipment by Stanton, had disbanded his regiment in early August; Rose, *Rehearsal*, pp. 189-98; U.S., War Department, *Official Register of Volunteer Forces*, pt. 8; Cornish, *Sable Arm*, p. 92.

## CHAPTER FOUR

1. James D. Richardson, *A Compilation of the Messages and Papers of the Presidents, 1789-1897* (10 vols., Washington, 1900), vol. 6, p. 158; *New York Times*, January 9, 1863, p. 4.

2. *O. R.*, ser. 3, vol. 3, p. 14.

3. *Orders and Letters of Brigadier General Daniel Ullmann, February to June, 1863*, MS, Generals' Papers and Books, War Records Division, National Archives.

4. U.S., Congress, *Senate Bills and Joint Resolutions* (Washington, 1863), 37th Congress, 3rd Session, 1862-63, pp. 5, 511; Leach, *Conscription*, pp. 165-66.

5. *New York Times*, February 16, 1863, p. 4.

6. *Washington Daily National Intelligencer*, February 28, 1863; *Congressional Globe* (Washington, 1861-67), 37th Congress, 3rd Session, pp. 976-78; Leach, *Conscription*, pp. 172-73.

7. *Congressional Globe*, 37th Congress, 3rd Session, pp. 978-79; Leach, *Conscription*, pp. 173-75.

8. *Congressional Globe*, 37th Congress, 3rd Session, pp. 181-83; Leach, *Conscription*, p. 178.

9. *Congressional Globe*, 37th Congress, 3rd Session, pp. 100-102; Leach, *Conscription*, pp. 187-88.

10. *Congressional Globe*, 37th Congress, 3rd Session, pp. 282, 690, 695, 924; Cornish, *Sable Arm*, p. 99.

11. *Congressional Globe*, 37th Congress, 3rd Session, pp. 1217-22; Leach, *Conscription*, pp. 712-93.

12. *Congressional Globe*, 37th Congress, 3rd Session, pp. 1224-78 passim; Leach, *Conscription*, pp. 194-96.

13. *Congressional Globe*, 37th Congress, 3rd Session, pp. 1271-93 passim; Leach, *Conscription*, pp. 205-7.

14. *Congressional Globe*, 37th Congress, 3rd Session, pp. 1363-68, 1371-80, 1384-89, 1419, 1423.

15. *Congressional Globe*, 37th Congress, 3rd Session, p. 1494; U.S., *Statutes at Large of the United States, 1789-1868*, vol. 12, pp. 73-77; Hyman, *More Perfect Union*, pp. 215, 221, (Hyman does not, however,

fit conscription into the framework of his discussion of federalism).

16. *New York Times*, February 2, 1863; February 26, 1863; March 7, 1863; March 26, 1863; *New York World*, February 2, 1863; March 5, 1863; Leach, *Conscription*, pp. 217-45.

17. John G. Nicolay and John Hay, *The Complete Works of Abraham Lincoln* (12 vols., New York, 1903), vol. 11, pp. 74-83.

18. Plumly to Banks, September 24, 1863, Banks Papers, Library of Congress; Nathaniel Emory to General Stone, October 6, 1863, Department of the Gulf, Record Group 393, National Archives; Orders and Letters of Brigadier General Lorenzo Thomas, April to November 24, 1863, MS, Generals' Papers and Books, War Records Division, National Archives; Cornish, *Sable Arm*, p. 111.

19. *O. R.*, ser. 3, vol. 3, p. 103, vol. 5, p. 66; Blassingame, *Black New Orleans*, pp. 37-38; Henry T. Johns, *Life with the Forty-Ninth Massachusetts Volunteers* (Pittsfield, Mass., 1864), p. 187; George Hanks to General Nathaniel Banks, August 5, 1863, Department of the Gulf, Record Group 393, National Archives.

20. Nicolay and Hay, *Works of Abraham Lincoln*, vol. 8, p. 233.

21. Ibid., pp. 318-19; *American Annual Cyclopaedia and Register of Important Events for the Year 1865, Embracing Political, Civil, Military and Social Affairs* (New York, 1869), p. 31, Report of Stanton to Congress; U.S., Adjutant General's Office, *Statement of Number of Men Called for and the Number Furnished from April 15, 1861, to Close of the War of Rebellion*, p. 3; Leach, *Conscription*, pp. 278-79; *New York Times*, April 21, 1863, p. 4, June 11, 1863, p. 2, June 13, 1863, p. 2; U.S. War Department, Generals' Papers and Reports, 1861-1865, vol. 14, pp. 131-33.

22. *Washington Daily National Intelligencer*, July 11, 1863, p. 2; *New York World*, July 11, 1863, p. 4; Henry G. Pearson, *The Life of John A. Andrew, Governor of Massachusetts, 1861-1865* (2 vols., Boston, 1904), vol. 2, pp. 134-35; Leach, *Conscription*, pp. 398-99.

23. John A. Logan, *The Great Conspiracy: Its Origin and History* (New York, 1886), p. 516; Leach, *Conscription*, p. 295; James McCague, *The Second Rebellion: The Story of the New York City Draft Riots, 1863* (New York, 1968).

24. *New York World*, July 14, 1863; *Washington Daily National Intelligencer*, July 16, 1863; Martha D. Perry, comp., *Letters from a Surgeon of the Civil War* (Boston, 1906); Leach, *Conscription*, pp. 301-2.

25. George Meade, *Life and Letters of George Gordon Meade* (2 vols., New York, 1913), vol. 2, p. 143; Rachel S. Thorndike, ed., *The Sherman Letters: Correspondence Between General and Senator Sherman, from 1837 to 1891* (New York, 1894), pp. 193-95; Leach, *Conscription*, pp. 347-48.

26. U.S., *Provost Marshal General's Final Report of March 17, 1866*, vol. 1, p. 40; Leach, *Conscription*, pp. 348-49.

CHAPTER FIVE

1. Louis Emilio, *History of the Fifty-Fourth Regiment of Massachusetts Volunteer Infantry, 1863-1865* (Boston, 1891), pp. 117-121; Berry, "Negro Troops in Blue and Grey," pp. 188-96; *O.R.*, ser. 3, vol. 3, p. 115; Blassingame, *Black New Orleans*, pp. 37, 41.
2. *New York Times*, May 20, 1863, p. 2, June 11, 1863, p. 2; *O.R.*, ser. 2, vol. 3, pp. 153-55, ser. 1, vol. 26, pt. 1, p. 234; Nicolay and Hay *Works of Abraham Lincoln*, vol. 9, p. 48.
3. *Washington Daily National Intelligencer*, August 6, 1863.
4. Nicolay and Hay, *Works of Abraham Lincoln*, vol. 9, pp. 37, 64-65; 99-116 passim.
5. *O.R.*, ser. 3, vol. 3, pp. 682-84, vol. 4, p. 764.
6. Quarles, *Negro in the Civil War*, p. 248.
7. *O.R.*, ser. 1, vol. 14, p. 377; U.S., *Statutes at Large*, vol. 12, pp. 592, 599.
8. *New York Times*, May 24, 1863, p. 4.
9. *O.R.*, ser. 3, vol. 3, pp. 252, 420; U.S., Congress, *House Executive Document No. 1* (Washington, 1864), 38th Congress, 1st Session, p. 8.
10. Thomas Wentworth Higginson, *Army Life in a Black Regiment* (Boston, 1890), pp. 283-84; *Chicago Tribune*, May 1, 1864; *Congressional Globe*, 38th Congress, 1st Session, p. 565; Cornish, *Sable Arm* pp. 191-92.
11. U.S., Congress, *House Executive Document No. 1*, 38th Congress, 1st Session; McPherson, *The Negro's Civil War*, p. 199; U.S. *Provost Marshal General's Final Report*, vol. 2, pp. 227-28; Thomas M. Cook, *Public Record of Horatio Seymour* (New York, 1868), pp. 164-65, 198-99; William D. Foulke, *Life of Oliver P. Morton* (2 vols., Indianapolis, 1899), vol. 1, pp. 201-2; Leach, *Conscription*, pp. 393-94.
12. *Congressional Globe*, 38th Congress, 1st Session, pp. 70, 94-95, 580-630; U.S., *Statutes at Large*, vol. 12, pp. 6-11, 18; Sherman, *Memoirs of William T. Sherman*, vol. 2, p. 116; Leach, *Conscription*, pp. 396-99.
13. Henry Wilson, *History of the Anti-Slavery Measures of the Thirty-Seventh and Thirty-Eighth Congresses, 1861-65* (Boston, 1865), pp. 293-94; Richard Henry Abbott, *Cobbler in Congress: The Life of Henry Wilson, 1812-1875* (Lexington, Ky., 1972), pp. 127, 133.
14. *Congressional Globe*, 38th Congress, 1st Session, p. 482; Wilson, *Anti-Slavery Measures*, pp. 295-96.
15. *Congressional Globe*, 38th Congress, 1st Session, pp. 566, 641-2, 770.
16. Ibid., pp. 870-71; Wilson, *Anti-Slavery Measures*, pp. 305-6.
17. *Congressional Globe*, 38th Congress, 1st Session, p. 1804; Wilson *Anti-Slavery Measures*, p. 306.
18. *Congressional Globe*, 38th Congress, 1st Session, pp. 1805, 1299-1306, 1308-14; Wilson, *Anti-Slavery Measures*, p. 307.
19. *Congressional Globe*, 38th Congress, 1st Session, pp. 1806, 1991, 1995-97; Wilson, *Anti-Slavery Measures*, p. 308.
20. *Congressional Globe*, 38th Congress, 1st Session, p. 2963; Wilson, *Anti-Slavery Measures*, p. 309.
21. *Congressional Globe*, 38th Congress, 1st Session, pp. 3040, 3063; Wilson, *Anti-Slavery Measures*, pp. 310-11.

22. McPherson, *Negro's Civil War*, p. 202; *Congressional Globe*, 38th Congress, 1st Session, pp. 564, 3086, 3116; Wilson, *Anti-Slavery Measures*, pp. 311-12.

23. Pearson, *Life of John A. Andrew*, vol. 2, pp. 105-11.

24. U.S., *Official Opinions of the Attorneys General*, vol. 11, pp. 37-42.

25. Nicolay and Hay, *Works of Abraham Lincoln*, vol. 10, p. 133; U.S., *Official Opinions of the Attorneys General*, vol. 11, pp. 55-58; Higginson, *Army Life in a Black Regiment*, pp. 287-89; U.S., *Statutes at Large*, vol. 13, p. 488.

26. National Anti-Slavery Standard, February 14, 1863; Joseph T. Wilson, *Black Phalanx: A History of the Negro Soldiers in the Wars of 1775, 1812, 1861-65* (Hartford, 1888), pp. 166-70; John Blassingame, "The Selection of Officers and Non-Commissioned Officers of Negro Troops in the Union Army, 1861-1865," *Negro History Bulletin* 30 (1967), 11.

27. Emilio, *History of the Fifty-Fourth Regiment*, pp. 7-18.

28. *O.R.*, ser. 1. vol. 16, pp. 808-9.

29. Emilio, *History of the Fifty-Fourth Regiment*, pp. 179-80, 268.

30. Letter Book, *Fifty-Fourth Regiment of Massachusetts Volunteers of African Descent*, September 19, 1864, R.G. 94, Adjutant General's Office, MS, NA.

## CHAPTER SIX

1. Robert F. Durden, *The Gray and the Black: The Confederate Debate on Emancipation* (Baton Rouge, 1972), pp. 270-73, 296; Louis Gerteis, *From Contraband to Freedman: Federal Policy Toward Southern Blacks, 1861-1865* (Westport, Conn., 1973), pp. 193-94.

2. W. E. B. DuBois, *Black Reconstruction in America* (New York, 1969, originally published 1935), see generally chap. 6.

3. Gerteis, *From Contraband to Freedman*, pp. 39, 45, 74, 93, 110, 123-27; Peter Kolchin, *First Freedom: The Responses of Alabama Blacks to Emancipation and Reconstruction* (Westport, Conn., 1974), pp. 30-48.

4. George P. Rawick, ed., *The American Slave: A Composite Autobiography* (Westport, Conn., 1792); slave narrative collection of Federal Writer's Project, 1936-38, vol. 19, p. 186, vol. 2, pp. 69, 224.

5. *St. Louis Daily Missouri Democrat*, September 2, November 18, and December 7, 1863; John W. Blassingame, "The Recruitment of Negro Troops in Missouri During the Civil War," *Missouri Historical Review* 58 (April 1964), 326-38. The families of slave soldiers of enemy ownership were freed, technically, under the Militia Act of July 17, 1862.

6. *St. Louis Daily Missouri Democrat*, January 5, 1864; U.S., War Department, *Digest of the Opinions of the Judge Advocate General of the Army* (Washington, 1865), p. 79; *Kansas City Daily Journal of Commerce*, December 4, 1863, January 21, 1864; Blassingame, "Recruitment of Negro Troops," pp. 326-38; Rawick, ed., *American Slave*, vol. 6, p. 79.

7. Wilson, *Anti-Slavery Measures*, pp. 313-14; Ernest McKay, *Henry Wilson, Practical Radical: Portrait of a Politician* (Port Washington, New York, 1971), pp. 184-85.
8. *Congressional Globe*, 38th Congress, 1st Session, pp. 362, 524.
9. Howard Devon Hamilton, "Legislative and Judicial History of the Thirteenth Amendment," pp. 1-10; *Congressional Globe*, 38th Congress, 1st Session, p. 521; Wilson, *Anti-Slavery Measures*, pp. 322, 324; Harold Hyman, *More Perfect Union*, pp. 270-71.
10. Wilson, *Anti-Slavery Measures*, pp. 326-27.
11. Ibid., pp. 346, 399, 401; Quarles, *Negro in the Civil War*, pp. 258-60; *Congressional Globe*, 38th Congress, 2nd Session, pp. 64, 113-15.
12. Wilson, *Anti-Slavery Measures*, pp. 403-04; Edward McPherson, *The Political History of the United States of America During the Great Rebellion, Including a Summary of Congressional Legislation* (Washington, 1865), p. 564; Paul J. Lammermeier, "The Urban Black Family of the Nineteenth Century: A Study of Black Family Structure in the Ohio Valley, 1850-1880," *Journal of Marriage and the Family* 35 (1973), 440-456; John W. Blassingame, *The Slave Community* (New York, 1972), chap. 3; Elizabeth H. Pleck, "The Two Parent Household: Black Family Structure in Late Nineteenth Century Boston," *Journal of Social History* 4 (Fall 1972), 3-31; *Corbin v. Marsh*, 2 Duvall, 193 (Kentucky, December, 1865); Patricia MacDonald, *Baltimore Women 1870-1900*. Ph. D. dissertation, University of Maryland (1976), Ch. III.
13. U.S., *Official Opinions of the Attorneys General of the United States Advising the President and Heads of Department of Their Official Duties and Expounding the Constitution, Treaties with Foreign Governments, and with Indian Tribes, and the Public Laws of the Country* (38 vols., Washington, 1852-), vol. 11, pp. 356-66, 369, 370-72.
14. See, for example, Muster-Out Rolls, First, Second, and Third Louisiana Native Guards, Fifty-Fourth and Fifty-Fifth Regiments of Massachusetts Volunteers of African Descent, Adjutant General's Office, Record Group 94, MS, National Archives; Emilio, *History of the Fifty-Fourth Regiment*, pp. 327-28; U.S., *Statutes at Large*, vol. 14, p. 357.

## CHAPTER SEVEN

1. Lawanda and John Cox, *Politics, Principle and Prejudice, 1856-66: Dilemma of Reconstruction America* (New York, 1963), p. 30; Howard Devon Hamilton, "The Legislative and Judicial History of the Thirteenth Amendment," Ph.D. dissertation, University of Illinois, 1950, pp. 1-10, discusses the introduction of five unsuccessful amendments into the Congress beginning with the bill of Representative James Ashley in December 1863; also in Charles Fairman, *Reconstruction and Reunion 1864-1888*; Oliver Wendell Holmes, *Devise History of the Supreme Court of the United States* (New York, 1971), pt. 1, pp. 1136-54; Jacobus Tenbroek, *Equal under Law* (New York, 1965), pp. 166, 167, 173, 46.
2. Joseph B. James, *The Framing of the Fourteenth Amendment* (Urbana, 1958), passim, esp. 184-85; Hamilton, "Thirteenth Amend-

ment," pp. 10, 20; Cox and Cox, *Politics, Principle and Prejudice*, pp. 13-16.

3. *Congressional Globe*, 38th Congress, 3rd Session, pp. 113-114; Hamilton, "Thirteenth Amendment," pp. 13-16.

4. *Congressional Globe*, 38th Congress, 2nd Session, p. 144.

5. Ibid., p. 170.

6. Ibid., p. 179; V. Jacques Voegeli, *Free but Not Equal: The Midwest and the Negro During the Civil War* (Chicago, 1967), pp. 174-77.

7. *Congressional Globe*, 38th Congress, 3rd Session, p. 224; Frank E. Klement, "Midwestern Opposition to Lincoln's Emancipation Policy," *Journal of Negro History* 49 (1964), 170-71.

8. *Congressional Globe*, 38th Congress, 3rd Session, pp. 240-41; Cox and Cox, *Politics, Principle and Prejudice*, p. 18.

9. *Congressional Globe*, 38th Congress, 3rd Session, pp. 531, 588; Cox and Cox, *Politics, Principle and Prejudice*, p. 25.

10. M. S. Littlefield to Lyman Trumbull, May 8, 1865; C. E. Lippincott to Trumbull, August 29, 1865, Lyman Trumbull Papers, reel 16, vol. 60, and reel 17, vol. 61, Library of Congress. See also S. Brisbane to Thaddeus Stevens, December 29, 1863, Thaddeus Stevens Papers, vol. 5, Library of Congress.

11. Hamilton, "Thirteenth Amendment," pp. 13-20; Richard Mendales, "Republican Defectors to the Democracy During Reconstruction," paper read at the November 1973 annual meeting of the Southern Historical Association, copy in my possession.

12. Hamilton, "Thirteenth Amendment," pp. 55-58; Robert L. Kohl, "The Civil Rights Act of 1866: Its Hour Come Round at Last, *Jones* v. *Alfred Mayer Co.*," *Virginia Law Review* 55 (1969), 272.

13. *O.R.*, ser. 3, vol. 5. p. 661; James Sefton, *The United States Army and Reconstruction, 1865-77* (Baton Rouge, 1967), pp. 50-52; John Hope Franklin, "Reconstruction and The Negro," in Harold Hyman, ed., *New Frontiers of Reconstruction Historiography* (Urbana, 1966), pp. 69-70; William F. Messner, "Black Violence and White Response," pp. 36-37, implies that whites regarded black soldiers as nonthreatening and docile by the end of the War.

14. Gillmore to Lorenzo Thomas, A.G., U.S.A., August 20, 1865, Department of the South, 15, R.G. 98, as quoted in Sefton, *Army and Reconstruction*, p. 52.

15. *O.R.*, ser. 3, vol. 5, p. 58, 108; Grant to Stanton and Stanton to Acting Assistant Secretary of War Major Thomas Eckert, September 6, 1865, vol. 28, Edwin Stanton Papers, Library of Congress.

16. Regimental Order Book, Third Louisiana Native Guard Infantry Regiment, R.G. 94, Adjutant General's Office, MS, NA: Letter Book, Fifty-Fourth Massachusetts Infantry, Regiment; R. Marsh to Stanton, January 28, 1865, Stanton Papers, vol. 24, Library of Congress.

17. Sefton, *Army and Reconstruction*, pp. 43-45; but c.f. Cox and Cox, *Politics, Principle and Prejudice*, p. 1, and John Hope Franklin, "Reconstruction and the Negro," pp. 69-70.

18. Lawanda Cox, "The Promise of Land for the Freedom," *Mississippi Valley Historical Review* 45 (1958), 413-39; Gerteis, *From Contraband to Freedman*, pp. 186-90 and notes there cited; Mary F. Berry,

"Reparations for Freedmen, 1890-1916: Fraudulent Practices or Justice Deferred," *Journal of Negro History* 58 (1972), 219-30.

19. Lee Soltow, "Economic Inequality in the United States in the Period from 1790 to 1860," *Journal of Economic History* 31 (1971), 822-39; Norman Ware, *The Industrial Worker, 1840-1860.*
20. Horace M. Bond, *The Education of the Negro in the American Social Order* (New York, 1934).
21. Phillip Foner, ed., *The Life and Writings of Frederick Douglass,* 4 vols. (New York, 1952), vol. 3, p. 343.
22. *New Orleans Tribune,* October 25, 1864.
23. Foner, *Life and Writings of Frederick Douglass,* vol. 3, pp. 418-20.
24. *Congressional Globe,* 39th Congress, 1st Session, pp. 47-48, 90-91; Fairman, *Reconstruction and Reunion,* pp. 104, 113-18, 465-68, pt. 1, pp. 1172-93; Kohl, "The Civil Rights Act of 1866," pp. 286-87.
25. *Congressional Globe,* 39th Congress, 1st Session, pp. 174, 178, 202-17, 504.
26. Ibid., p. 322; Robert S. Kaczorowski, "Searching for the Intent of the Framers of the Fourteenth Amendment, " *Connecticut Law Review* 5 (1972-73), 368; Kaczorowski believes that civil rights in the 1866 act were meant to include the natural rights of freedmen, the rights to life, liberty, and property (379-84); but c.f. Hamilton, "Thirteenth Amendment," pp. 59-61, and Fairman, *Reconstruction and Reunion,* pt. 1, pp. 1216-37, on the intent of the framers, discussed within a criticism of the Supreme Court's decision in *Jones* v. *Alfred Mayer Co.* 392, U.S. 409 (1968), in which the Court decided that the Civil Rights Act of 1866 barred private racial discrimination in housing and was a valid exercise of authority under the Thirteenth Amendment. They agree with a narrow interpretation of the Thirteenth Amendment and the act. A short analysis very similar to Fairman's may be found in Senator Sam J. Ervin, Jr. *"Jones* v. *Alfred H. Mayer and Co.*: Judicial Activism Run Riot," *Vanderbilt Law Review* 22 (1969), 485, and Justice Harlan's opinion in the *Jones* case. For a contrary view, see Kohl, "The Civil Rights Act of 1866," pp. 292-300.
27. Michael Benedict, "Preserving the Constitution: The Conservative Basis of Radical Reconstruction," *Journal of American History* 61 (1974), 65-90; Michael Perman, *Reunion Without Compromise.*
28. House Doc. 72, 39th Congress, 2nd session, Letters of Secretary of War, January 21, 1867, Sen. Doc. 209, 57th Congress, 2nd Session (1903), pp. 108-11; House Report 101, 39th Congress, 1st session (1866), p. 36; Sefton, *Army and Reconstruction,* p. 82; Berry, *Black Resistance,* pp. 93-94.
29. David C. Rankin, "The Origins of Black Leadership in New Orleans During Reconstruction," *Journal of Southern History* 40 (1974), 417-40 and notes there cited. Most of the Negro leaders of New Orleans after the war had served in the army and had ties of education, family, and blood to a sophisticated and exclusive community. In South Carolina, black Union veterans Martin Delany, L. S. Langley, William Whipper, and Stephen Swails stayed in the state and held state political offices during Reconstruction; Joel Williamson, *After Slavery: The Negro in South Carolina During Reconstruction, 1861-1877* (Chapel

Hill, 1965), pp. 28-30, 330; Okon Edet Uya, *From Slavery to Public Service: Robert Smalls, 1839-1915* (New York, 1971).

30. Michael Benedict, *A Compromise of Principle: Congressional Republicans and Reconstruction, 1863-1869* (New York, 1974), pp. 164, 170, 222, 331, and notes there cited.

31. Otis Singletary, *The Negro Militia and Reconstruction* (Austin, 1957), pp. 9, 24, 129, 145-46.

# BIBLIOGRAPHICAL ESSAY

The most complete collection of unpublished primary materials relating to blacks in the army for the period covered is "The Negro in the Military Service of the United States: A compilation of official records, state papers, historical records, 1639-1886," 5 vols., in the National Archives. Additional useful materials in the National Archives in Record Group 94, Adjutant General's Office, Colored Troops Division records are muster rolls, morning reports, and carded military service records of black troops during the Civil War. In the War Records Division of the National Archives, General's Reports of Service Orders and Letters of Brigadier Generals Lorenzo Thomas and Daniel Ullman and the Department of the Gulf Provost Marshal General's Records provide detailed information concerning many aspects of black military life.

In the Manuscript Division of the Library of Congress the papers of Nathaniel Banks, Salmon P. Chase, James Doolittle, Edwin Stanton, Thaddeus Stevens, and Lyman Trumbull provide valuable information concerning War Department policy and congressional attitudes. In the Howard University Library the papers of P. B. S. Pinchback and several master's theses on blacks in the military service contain significant information on the attitudes of blacks toward their service.

The most useful government publications are the statutes and records of legislative debates in England and the several colonies and states found in the Library of Congress Law Library and the University of Michigan Law Library. Also Clarence Carter, ed., *Territorial Papers of the United States* (18 vols., Washington, 1934) contains a wealth of material on blacks and the military service in Louisiana before and after the Louisiana Purchase. The official development of national military enlistment law can be followed by using James D. Richardson, *A Compilation of the Messages and Papers of the Presidents, 1789-1897* (10 vols., Washington, 1900), *The Statutes at Large of the United States, The Journals of the Continental Congress, The Annals of Congress, The Congressional Globe,* and the *Congressional Record.* Additionally *The Records of the Provost Marshal General of the U.S. War Department, American State Papers, Military Affairs,* the *Official Opinions of the Attorneys General of the United States,* and the volumes entitled *War of the Rebellion: A Compilation of the Official Records of the Union and Confederate Armies* provide a wealth of evidence of law and practice.

For the Colonial and Revolutionary periods a number of diaries and memoirs including Charles Francis Adams, ed., John Adams's *Works* (10 vols., Boston, 1850-56), Edmund Burnett, ed., *Letters of Members of the Continental Congress* (8 vols., Washington, 1921-36), Jonathan Elliott, ed., *The Debates in the Several State Conventions on the Adoption of the Federal Constitution* (5 vols., Philadelphia, 1861), John C. Fitzpatrick, *The Writings of George Washington from the Original Manuscript Sources, 1745-1792* (30 vols., Washington, 1931-34), Leonard Labaree, ed., *The Papers of Benjamin Franklin* (New Haven, 1959), John B. McMaster and Frederick D. Stone, eds., *Pennsylvania and the Federal Constitution, 1787-1788* (Lancaster, Pa. 1888), *Frank Moore's Diary of the American Revolution* (2 vols., New York, 1865), and Edward Tatum, ed., *The American Journal of Ambrose Serle, Secretary to Lord Howe, 1776-1778* (San Marino, Calif., 1940), are most helpful.

For the period from the Constitution to the beginning of the Civil War, Henry Adams, ed., *Documents Relating to New England Federalism* (Boston, 1870), John S. Bassett, ed., *The Correspondence of Andrew Jackson* (7 vols., Washington, 1926-1935), Samuel E. Morison, *The Life and Letters of Harrison Gray Otis, Federalist, 1765-1848* (2 vols., Boston, 1913), Dunbar Rowland, ed., *Official Letter Books of W. C. C. Claiborne, 1801-1816,* provide valuable material.

On Civil War developments, significant evidence on policy and attitudes in the Executive Branch is found in Roy Basler, ed., *Collected Works of Abraham Lincoln* and *Abraham Lincoln, His Speeches and Writings* (8 vols., New Brunswick, N. J., 1853-1855), John G. Nicolay and John Hay, *Complete Works of Abraham Lincoln* (12 vols., New York, 1905), and *Abraham Lincoln: A History* (10 vols., New York, 1890), George Baker, ed., *The Works of William H. Seward* (5 vols., Boston, 1884), Howard Beale, ed., *The Diary of Edward Bates, 1859-1866* (Washington, 1953), and David Donald, ed., *Inside Lincoln's Cabinet: The Civil War Diaries of Salmon P. Chase* (New York, 1954). Important recollections of military participants include *The Private and Official Correspondence of General*

*Benjamin F. Butler During the Period of the Civil War* (5 vols., Norwood, Mass., 1917), John W. DeForest's, *A Volunteer's Adventures: A Union Captain's Record of the Civil War*, ed. by James Croushore (New Haven, 1946), Richard Thorndike, ed., *The Sherman Letters: Correspondence Between General and Senator Sherman from 1837-1879* (New York, 1894), Joseph T. Wilson, *Black Phalanx: A History of the Negro Soldiers in the Wars of 1775, 1812, 1861-1865* (Hartford, Conn., 1888), Salmon P. Chase, *Diary and Correspondence* (Washington, 1903), Luis F. Emilio, *History of the Fifty-Fourth Regiment of Massachusetts Volunteer Infantry, 1863-1865* (Boston, 1891), Phillip Foner, ed., *The Life and Writings of Frederick Douglass* (4 vols., New York, 1952), Thomas W. Higginson, *Army Life in a Black Regiment* (Boston, 1900), Martha D. Perry, comp., *Letters from a Surgeon of the Civil War* (Boston, 1906), and Kate M. Rowland, ed., *The Journal of Julia LeGrand* (Richmond, 1911).

The newspapers are a valuable source for a number of the salient quotes and evidence of public opinion on the question of black eligibility for service and the prospects for the enactment of civil rights. The *Boston Daily Advertiser*, the *Boston Evening Transcript*, and the *Boston Morning Journal*; the *New York Times*, the *New York World Tribune*, and the *New York Evening Post*; the *New Orleans Daily Picayune*, *Daily True Delta* and *La Tribune*; the *Cincinnati Daily Commercial*; the *St. Louis Daily Missiouri Democrat*; the *Kansas City Daily Journal of Commerce*; the *Washington Daily National Intelligencer*; and the *Liberator* and the *National Antislavery Standard* provide a wide range of geographical and ideological perspectives.

There are several secondary accounts of blacks in the military service; Jack D. Foner, *Blacks and the Military in American History* (Washington, D. C., 1974) is the most recent and comprehensive. On the relationship between citizenship and the militia obligation, John H. Mahon, *The American Militia Decade of Decision, 1789-1800* (University of Florida Press, 1960) and Jack F. Leach, *Conscription in the United States: Historical Background* (Rutland, Vt., 1952) provide important background information.

On the subject of legal status and the military use of blacks in the colonial period, Benjamin Quarles, "The Colonial Militia and Negro Manpower," *Mississippi Valley Historical Review* 45 (1959), 513-21, and John W. Shy, "A New Look at Colonial Militia," *William and Mary Quarterly* 20 (1963), 175-85 are the most significant studies. Lindsay Boynton, *The Elizabethan Militia, 1588-1638* (London, 1976), Charles W. Hollister, *Anglo-Saxon Military Institutions on the Eve of the Norman Conquest* (Oxford, 1962), and John R. Western, *The English Militia in the Eighteenth Century: The Story of a Political Issue, 1660-1802* (London, 1965) describe the legal distinctions between service in the militia and the regulars in England. The essays in David W. Cohen and Jack P. Greene, eds., *Neither Slave Nor Free: The Freedmen of African Descent in the Slave Societies of the New World* (Baltimore, 1972), provide important material conerning military policy toward blacks in the British, French, Spanish, and Portuguese colonies.

For the Revolutionary period, Benjamin Quarles, *The Negro in the American Revolution* (Chapel Hill, 1961), Pete Mazlowski, "National Policy Toward the Use of Black Troops in the Revolution," *South Carolina Historical Magazine* 73 (January 1972), pp. 1-17, and Donald Robinson, *Slavery in the Structure of American Politics, 1765-1820* (Ithaca, 1971) provide the most useful analysis of the issues.

On the subject of black legal status and the obligation to perform military service between the Revolution and the Civil War, John Hope Franklin, *The Militant South, 1800-1861* (Cambridge, 1956), Robert J. Gough, "Black Men and the Early New Jersey Militia," *New Jersey History* 88 (Winter 1970), pp. 227-38, Leon Litwack, *North of Slavery* (Chicago, 1961), Benjamin Quarles, *Black Abolitionists* (New York, 1969), Ira Berlin, *Slaves Without Masters: The Free Negro in the Antebellum South* (New York, 1974), Roland C. McConnell, *Negro Troops in Ante-Bellum Louisiana* (Baton Rouge, 1968), James H. Pease and William H. Pease, *They Who Would Be Free* (New York, 1974), offer significant discussions of the issues.

The literature on the Civil War period is voluminous. Dudley Taylor Cornish, *The Sable Arm: Negro Troops in the Union Army, 1861-1865* (New York, 1956), and Benjamin Quarles, *The Negro in the Civil War* (Boston, 1953) are the most important studies of black participation in the War. V. Jacque Voegeli, *Free But Not Equal: The Midwest and the Negro During the Civil War* (Chicago, 1967), Harold Hyman, *A More Perfect Union* (New York, 1973), James G. Randall, *Constitutional Problems Under Lincoln* (New York, 1926), Emory Upton, *The Military Policy of the United States* (Washington, 1917), Robert F. Durden, *The Gray and the Black: The Confederate Debate on Emancipation* (Baton Rouge, 1972), Louis Gerteis, *From Contraband to Freedmen: Federal Policy Toward Southern Blacks, 1861-1865* (Westport, Conn., 1973), John W. Blassingame, "The Recruitment of Negro Troops in Missouri During the Civil War," *Missouri Historical Review* 58 (April 1964), pp. 326-338, and "The Selection of Officers and Non-commissioned Officers of Negro Troops in the Union Army, 1863-1865," *Negro History Bulletin* 30 (January, 1967), pp. 8-11, John W. Blassingame and Mary F. Berry, "Negro Troops in Blue and Gray: The Louisiana Native Guards, 1861-1863," *Louisiana History* 8 (Spring 1967), pp. 168-90, are the most significant studies of aspects of the development of federal enlistment policy and the question of the legal status of blacks.

A number of studies contain useful information concerning black attitudes and civil rights expectations. George P.Rawick, ed., *The American Slave: A Composite Autobiography* (Westport, Conn., 1972), the slave narrative collection of the Federal Writer's Project, James McPherson, *The Negro's Civil War: How American Negroes Felt and Acted During the War for the Union* (New York, 1965); Peter Kolchin, *First Freedom: The Responses of Alabama Blacks to Emancipation and Reconstruction* (Westport, Conn., 1974), John W. Blassingame, *The Slave Community* (New York, 1972), and Mary F. Berry "Reparations for Freedmen," *Journal of Negro History* 57 (1972), pp. 219-30, are most helpful.

Lawanda and John Cox, *Politics, Principle and Prejudice, 1865-66: Dilemma of Reconstruction America* (New York, 1963), John Hope Franklin, "Reconstruction and the Negro," in Hyman, ed., *New Frontiers of Reconstruction Historiography* (Urbana, 1966), Jacobus Ten Broek, *Equal Under Law* (New York, 1965), Joseph B. James, *The Framing of the Fourteenth Amendment* (Urbana, 1958) are essential for interpreting the origins of the Thirteenth and Fourteenth amendments. Michael Les Benedict, *A Compromise of Principle: Congressional Republicans and Reconstruction* (New York, 1974), Phillip S. Paludan, *A Covenant with Death: The Constitution, Law and Equality in the Civil War Era* (Urbana, Ill., 1975), Charles Fairman, *Reconstruction and Reunion, 1864-1888* (New York, 1971), Robert J. Kaczorowski, "Searching for the Intent of the Framers of the Fourteenth Amendment," *Connecticut Law Review* 5 (1972-73), pp. 348-68, and Herman Belz, *Reconstructing the Union* (Ithaca, N. Y., 1969) help to clarify the public policy developments.

James Sefton, *The United States Army and Reconstruction, 1865-1877* (Baton Rouge, 1967), and Otis Singletary, *The Negro Militia and Reconstruction* (Austin, 1957) are the most important studies of the military use of blacks and the attitudes of whites in the service during Reconstruction.

On the post-war political activities of black veterans, David C. Rankin, "The Origins of Black Leadership in New Orleans During Reconstruction," *Journal of Southern History* 40 (1974), pp. 417-40; Joel Williamson, *After Slavery: The Negro in South Carolina During Reconstruction, 1861-1877* (Chapel Hill, 1965), Okon Edet Uya, *From Slavery to Public Service: Robert Smalls, 1839-1915* (New York, 1971), John W. Blassingame, *Black New Orleans, 1860-1880* (Chicago, 1974), and Samuel D. Smith, *The Negro in Congress, 1870-1901* (Chapel Hill, 1940) provide useful information.

# INDEX

Army, Revolutionary, blacks in, 9, 13
Army, U. S., 22, 25, 26; blacks in Union
    Army, 37, 39, 40-41, 42-45, 47,
    50-56, 58, 61, 62, 72-73, 80, 83;
    blacks in War of 1812, 29-30; number
    of blacks in, 75, 77, 84, 89, 90, 91,
    106; service in, 34, 35; U. S. Colored
    Troops, 56, 61, 62, 64
Articles of Confederation, 8-9
Attucks, Crispus, 8

Bates, Edward, 70-71, 82
Battle of Bull Run, 35
Battle of Bunker Hill, 10
Black, aims in Civil War, 94, 95; and
    Declaration of Independence, 12;
    attitude of in Civil War, 46, 49;
    battalion at Valley Forge, 13, 31;
    bill to promote enlistment of, 79-81;
    condition of in Civil War, 76-79;
    drafted, 57, 78-79; equal pay bill,
    65-71, 73; excluded from U. S.
    militia, 22, 23, 25, 27; family stability,
    82; fear of arming, 36; fear of in
    American colonies, 4, 5, 10-11; fear
    of in Louisiana, 25, 28; fear of in
    South, 31, 92; in colonial New Eng-
    land, 4; in colonial South, 4, 5, 9, 12,
    13, 14, 15; in Louisiana militia, 16,
    23-24, 25, 27-28, 29, 33, 102; in
    Massachusetts, 32, 33; in Revolution-
    ary War, 9, 13; in Union Army, 37,
    39, 40-41, 42, 43, 44, 45, 47, 50-56,
    58, 61, 62, 72-73, 80, 83; in War of
    1812, 25, 26, 27, 29; land for freed,
    78; lynched, 59; males in militia, 35,
    41; mustering out of army, 91-92;
    number of in Union Army, 75, 77,

84, 89, 90-91; objects of prejudice,
    3, 12, 30-31, 47, 76, 90; refugee
    camps for, 76, 77; restricted from
    U. S. Army, 30, 36; veterans'
    benefits for, 29; women as
    nurses, 29
Black Code of 1724, 7
Black codes, 98
Black prisoners of war, 62
Black sailors, 22, 30, 84
Black suffrage, 85-86, 90, 96-97, 98
Black women as nurses, 29
Bureau of Colored Troops, 56, 61,
    62, 64
Butler, Benjamin, 37-38, 45-46, 47,
    50, 72, 76

Calhoun, John, 30
Civil rights, 8, 85-86
Civil Rights Act of 1866, 85-86, 90,
    91, 96, 105; reaction to in South,
    97-98
Civil War, black troops in, 61-65,
    72-73, 76-77, 78-80, 83, 103;
    draft during, 50-58; draft riots
    in, 58-59; fugitive slaves in,
    76-77; end of, 84, 99; militia in,
    34-46; equal pay bill for black
    troops in, 65, 71-73. See also
    Army; Blacks
Claiborne, William C., 23-25, 27
Colonial period, 1-19, 100
Confederate States of America, 37,
    39, 45, 53, 61, 75, 84
Confiscation Act of 1861, 36, 38, 40.
    See also Second Confiscation Act
Congress. See U. S. Congress
Conscription, 26-27, 44, 48